TRUMPING PHILOSOPY

THE GREATEST MIND EXPLAINS THE GREATEST MINDS

COPYRIGHT PAGE

All rights reserved. No part of this publication may be republished in any form or by any means, including photocopying, scanning or otherwise without prior written permission to the copyright holder.

Copyright © [2023] by Chat TCT.

[JOIN MY MAILING LIST](#) for updates on future works by Chat TCT. Next up: Trumping Mathematics: the Greatest Mind Explains the Greatest Cosines

Join here: subscribepage.io/8szqpX

Dedicated to the Plan II Honors Program at the University of Texas at Austin, especially Dr. Woodruff, Dr. Solomon and Dr. Kane. My apologies!

TABLE OF CONTENT

INTRODUCTION 7

PYTHAGORAS 9

CONFUCIUS 11

HERACLEITUS 13

PARMENIDES 15

ZENO 17

SOCRATES 20

DEMOCRITUS 22

PLATO 24

ARISTOTLE 26

MENCIUS 28

ZHUANGZI 30

PYRRHON OF ELIS 33

EPICURUS 35

ZENO OF CITIUM 37

PHILO OF JUDAEUS 39

EPICTETUS 41

MARCUS AURELIUS 43

NAGARJUNA 45

PLOTINUS 47

SEXTUS EMPIRICUS 49

SAINT AUGUSTINE 51

HYPATIA 53

SANKARA 55

AL-FARABI	58
AVICENNA	60
RAMANUJA	62
SOLOMON IBN GABIROL	64
AL-GHAZALI	66
PETER ABELARD	68
AVERROES	70
ZHU-XI	72
MAIMONIDES	74
IBN AL-ARABI	76
SHINRAN	78
SAINT THOMAS AQUINAS	80
JON DUNS SCOTUS	82
WILLIAM OF OCKHAM	84
MACHIAVELLI	86
WANG YANGMING	88
FRANCIS BACON	90
THOMAS HOBBES	93
RENE DESCARTES	95
JOHN LOCKE	97
BENEDICT DE SPINOZA	99
LEIBNIZ	101
GIAMBATTISTA VICO	103
GEORGE BERKELEY	105
CHARLES LOUIS DE SECONDAT	107
DAVID HUME	109
ROUSSEAU	111

KANT	113
MOSES MENDELSSOHN	115
MARQUIS DE CONDORCET	117
JEREMY BENTHAM	119
HEGEL	121
SCHOPENHAUER	123
COMTE	125
JOHN STEWART MILL	127
KIERKEGAARD	129
KARL MARX	131
HERBERT SPENCER	133
WILLIAM DILTHEY	135
WILLIAM JAMES	137
NIETZSCHE	139
FREGE	141
EDMUND HUSSERL	143
HENRI BERGSON	145
JOHN DEWEY	147
ALFRED NORTH WHITEHEAD	149
BENEDETTO CROCE	151
NISHIDA KITARO	153
BERTRAND RUSSELL	155
GE MOORE	157
MARTIN BUBER	159
WITTGENSTEIN	161
HEIDEGGER	163
RUDOLPH CARNAP	165

KARL POPPER	167
THEODORE ADORNO	169
JEAN-PAUL SARTRE	171
HANNAH ARENDT	172
SIMONE DE BEAUVOIR	174
WILLARD VAN ORMAN QUINE	176
AJ AYER	178
WILFRID SELLARS	180
JOHN RAWLS	182
THOMAS S. KUHN	184
FOUCALT	186
NOAM CHOMSKY	188
JURGEN HABERMAS	190
SIR BERNARD WILLIAMS	192
JACQUES DERRIDA	194
RICHARD RORTY	196
ROBERT NOZICK	198
SAUL KRIPKE	200
DAVID KELLOGG LEWIS	201
PETER SINGER	203
PAUL WOODRUFF	205
ROBERT KANE	207
ROBERT SOLOMON	209
ABOUT THE AUTHOR	212

INTRODUCTION

Ladies and gentlemen, firstly, let me say thank you for being here. This is perhaps one of the greatest crowds ever assembled, and that's because of the power of books. I can't see all of you, but believe me, I know this is a tremendous group, tremendous. Now, let me tell you something. Nobody knows philosophy better than me. Believe me, I've got a tremendous mind, the best mind. And that's why I wrote this incredible book, "Trumping Philosophy: The Greatest Mind Explains the Greatest Minds." It's a huge honor to be here and share my wisdom with you.

Now, philosophy, it's a big word, it's a fancy word. But let me make it simple. Philosophy is really just about thinking, and let me tell you, nobody thinks better than me. I think so big, you won't even believe it. People come up to me and say, "Donald, how do you come up with these amazing thoughts?" And I say to these people, "It's simple, folks, I've got a very, very, very, very, very, very big brain."

Now, some people— and frankly, these people are not very smart, they couldn't figure this out on their own— some people might say, "But Donald, philosophy is complicated." Well, I'm here to tell you that's fake news. Philosophy is easy, especially when you have the world's best very stable genius to explain it all to you. I'm going to simplify these philosophers' ideas like you've never seen before. It's going to be tremendous, believe me.

In this tremendous book, you're gonna go on a journey through the minds of the greatest philosophers in history. Socrates, Aristotle, Plato, we've got 'em all. We've got some of the best, and some of the worst. We're talking about some serious heavyweights here, on both sides, very fine people. But you know what? They're no match for me. I'm going to break down their ideas, their theories, and show you how I would do it better. Because, let's be honest, nobody does it better than me. Nobody.

So, get ready to delve into the greatest minds in history. We're going to talk about truth, ethics, politics, all the big stuff that these guys somehow made a living talking about. And by the time you finish this book, you'll have the best philosophies, folks. So, let's make philosophy great again. Thank you, God bless you, and God bless the United States of America!

Pythagoras

Let me tell you something, folks, Pythagoras, fantastic guy, a real winner. You know, people are talking about Pythagoras, and some of them are saying some very nice things, and some of them are saying, well some not so nice things, but that's okay. Smart people who understand him, people like you—they're saying he's got this incredible theorem, the Pythagorean theorem, and let me tell you, it's a beautiful thing. Nobody knows triangles better than Pythagoras, believe me.

So, here's the deal with Pythagoras, folks. He's got this theorem that says, "In a right-angled triangle, the square of the hypotenuse is equal to the sum of the squares of the other two sides." It's a powerful statement, very powerful, very American. It's all about those sides, folks, and how they relate to each other. And let me tell you, it's tremendous. When you take a look at what's going on in our country, all the horrible things in our cities, that side of our country is related to the left side as they bring in the crime and the drugs. Who knew we could've predicted this? Oh yeah, I did, and apparently so did Pythagoras.

Now, I've seen a lot of triangles in my time, and I gotta say, Pythagoras really nailed it with this one. He's got these squares, and he's got these sides, and they all come together in this amazing equation. It's like magic, folks, pure magic. It's not quite pure magic though. They didn't actually have that back in Greece, which was news to me and I think news to a lot of other people. But look, nobody does triangles better than Pythagoras, believe me, even if it's not magic.

And you know what's great about Pythagoras? He didn't just stop at triangles. He had this whole philosophy, this idea that numbers rule the universe. And you know what? I agree with him. Numbers are tremendous. They're everywhere, folks, and they're so important. I wouldn't have gotten anywhere in business without numbers. When you take a look at what I've done, you can see how numbers rule everything and how big and beautiful and American they can be. They can be used for some very bad things, too, like how Sleepy Joe and the Democrats changed the numbers in the voting machines.

So, there you have it, folks, Pythagoras and his incredible theorem. It's all about those sides, those squares, and the power of numbers. A real winner, that Pythagoras. He's a smart guy, folks, and we should all be thankful for his tremendous contributions to geometry.

Confucius

Alright, folks, listen up. We're gonna talk about China. Now, I know China. I love China. I've done many great deals with China, and I like to think that the greatest thing my administration did was make sure China wasn't ripping us off. But back in the day, they had this guy named Confucius. Now, let me tell you, Confucius, he's a tremendous guy, okay? He's a Chinese philosopher, supposedly a wise man. But let me tell you, I know a thing or two about wisdom, folks. I've got the best words, believe me.

So, Confucius, he had this whole thing about ethics and morality, talking about respect for elders, family values, and all that stuff. I gotta say, he was right on it. I mean, take a look at the Trump Organization. A family business. Ivanka and Eric, just wonderful and smart people. Barron, growing into a fine young man. Don Jr. He's there too. And as for respecting elders? Well, my mother was born in Scotland, and when you take a look at all the beautiful Trump golf courses there, what does that say other than respect?

Confucius had this idea of the "Golden Rule" - treat others the way you want to be treated. Well, let me tell you, folks, I've got my own rule, the Trump Rule. It goes like this: treat others the way they treat you. It's all about strength and being tough, folks. We can't let people walk all over us, right? And I've raised my kids that way, too. No one walks all over them except me.

Now, Confucius talked a lot about education and self-improvement. But a very stable genius such as your favorite president doesn't need to read all those books to know what's what. I trust my gut, and it's never steered me wrong. When I think of self-improvement, I think of dreaming more and building more.

So, yeah, Confucius had his ideas, but let me tell you, folks, I've made deals, I've built buildings, I've been in the spotlight. I'm a winner.

Heracleitus

Listen folks, I gotta tell you, this guy Heracleitus, what a LOSER! He goes around saying all this stuff about how everything is always changing and that you can't step in the same river twice. What is he even talking about? I mean, the water is still there, right? It's just moving. That's not change, that's just movement. Plus, if I can run faster than the water is flowing—and I can, believe me, I was a star athlete back in the day -Ted Dobias said best he ever coached—then I CAN run over it twice. This is what the fake news media wants you to believe, folks!

And let me tell you, this guy has no sense of style. He's always talking about fire and how it's the fundamental element of the universe. Fire, really? For Antifa, maybe. I prefer gold, or maybe marble. Those are elements that really make a statement. Fire just burns things down, it's not even that impressive. You can't build Trump Tower out of fire.

Plus, he's always saying these cryptic things like "the road up and the road down are one and the same." What does that even mean? I like things to be straightforward and clear, not all this weird riddle stuff. It's not even true. I've taken Pennsylvania Avenue both directions, and one way takes you to the Capitol, and the other just takes you to the highway! And he's always talking about how opposites are really the same thing. Like light and dark, or hot and cold. I don't buy it. You can't tell me that being in a hot tub is the same as being in a cold pool. That's just crazy talk. And you look at someone as wonderful as me and someone as sleepy and corrupt as Joe; there's nothing similar there at all!

And get this, he thinks that you can't trust your senses! Can you believe it? He's all like, "you can't step into the same river twice, because your senses are always deceiving you." Sorry buddy, but my senses are the best senses. Nobody has better senses than me. I have the best eyes, the best ears, the best nose, and as I told Little Marco, the best, well, everything. I know what I'm seeing, hearing, and smelling, believe me. I can see and smell bull for sure, and that's what this is, folks, loud and clear.

In conclusion, Heracleitus is a total disaster, and if he were alive today, he'd be one of the disastrous do-nothing Democrats. He's always talking nonsense, he has no sense of style, and he doesn't even trust his own senses. Sad!

Parmenides

Ok folks, I gotta tell ya, this Parmenides guy, he's a real philosopher, believe me. He's been around for a long time, thousands of years, and he's still famous, can you believe it? You know, this great country hasn't even been around that long. Sleepy Joe isn't even that old! Now, Parmenides had this crazy idea that existence never changes. Sounds pretty wild, right? But you know what, maybe he's right, maybe everything is unchanging, I mean look at my hair, it's been the same for years.

And let me tell you, Parmenides was also a big believer in reason, he thought that reason was the only way to find the truth. And you know what, I agree with him. I'm a very reasonable guy, the most reasonable, and that's why I always make the best decisions. I mean, look at my decision to run for president, it was a very reasonable decision, and it worked out great, believe me. Then you look at what we did in office, very reasonable policies, too! The other side, they aren't reasonable at all!

But here's the thing, Parmenides also believed that the senses can't be trusted. He thought that what we see and feel is just an illusion. And you know what, I gotta disagree with him on that one. You gotta trust your gut. I mean, have you seen me on TV? I'm the most handsome guy. And when I'm talking to people, they can feel my tremendous energy, and they know I'm the best, believe me. When you see me on TV, you can always believe what you're seeing, except when you CAN'T like on phony CNN and MSNBC!

Now, some people—some very nasty people— they say Parmenides was just spouting nonsense, and they call it the "paradox of change." But I don't buy it. Not at all. They're just trying to overcomplicate things, but it's really simple, believe me. Things change, but they're still the same. It's like my policies, they're changing, but they're still the best policies. You know who talked about change, folks? Obama! Look at how he changed the country and all the work we had to do to bring it back! Look at Dominion, changing votes! Bad news!

Parmenides was a pretty smart guy, but there were some thing's he was not-so-smart about. And that's okay; nobody's perfect, even me if you can believe it or not. Sometimes, I've made mistakes— you know, I really should have taken more credit for all the wonderful things I did for the country. But you know what, I think he'd be proud of me, because I'm also a big believer in reason, and I always stick to my beliefs, even if some people don't like it. So, let's give it up for Parmenides, folks, a great philosopher. He would've been a wonderful Republican, believe me.

Zeno

Okay, so Zeno was this Greek philosopher guy who had some pretty wacky ideas. He was obsessed with motion, and he came up with all these crazy paradoxes to prove that motion was actually impossible.

Now, some of you people might say, "Hey, that's stupid! Of course, things move!" But not Zeno. He was convinced that if you really thought about it, you'd realize that motion was just an illusion.

One of his most famous paradoxes was called the Achilles and the Tortoise paradox. Basically, he said that if Achilles and a tortoise were in a race, and the tortoise got a head start, Achilles could never catch up to him. Why? Because by the time Achilles got to where the tortoise had started, the tortoise would have moved a little bit further ahead. And by the time Achilles got to that new spot, the tortoise would have moved even further ahead. And so on and so on, ad infinitum.

Now, I know what you're thinking: "What kind of nonsense is that? Of course, Achilles can catch up to the tortoise!" But that's just because you're not as smart as Zeno. He was a really smart guy. Trust me.

Think about it like this, folks. Imagine a race between me, your favorite president, and the Democrats on their witch hunt. They keep trying to find something, anything really, and they dig and dig but they don't have anything! They're racing after me but they just can't catch me because there's nothing there. No matter how fast they run to make things up to catch me, no one believes them except the lame-stream media! I have the head start because real Americans like you know that I've done nothing wrong! See! It's an illusion!

Anyway, Zeno came up with a bunch of other paradoxes too, like the Dichotomy paradox and the Arrow paradox. But they all boil down to the same thing: motion is impossible.

So, why am I telling you all this? Well, I'm not really sure. Maybe it's because Zeno was a winner, just like me. He knew how to think outside the box, even if that meant coming up with some weird ideas that nobody else understood. And that's okay. A lot of very not-so-smart people on the Left didn't understand what I was trying to do, and that's why I made them so mad. Small brains. Sad!

But one thing's for sure: Zeno would have loved Twitter. He could have spent all day arguing with people about his paradoxes and driving them crazy. It would have been tremendous.

So, let's all take a page out of Zeno's book and start thinking outside the box. Who knows what kind of crazy ideas we'll come up with? A lot of people said that I'd never be able to be president, and now I'm without a doubt—except maybe with the exception of Lincoln— the greatest in this country's history. Maybe we'll even be able to prove that motion is impossible. You never know.

Socrates

Socrates, what can I say? You know, they're always talking about how he's just the best, but the truth is, everybody knows the guy's a total loser. Kind of like some presidents. He walks around Athens, talking to people all day, pretending like he's some kind of genius philosopher. But let me tell you, folks, he doesn't know anything. Believe me, I know about being a genius, okay?

So, Socrates thinks he's smart, but all he does is ask questions. That's his whole thing, just asking questions. He never has any answers, never has any solutions. It's like he's afraid to take a stand on anything. If he were alive today, he'd be a RINO. Sad!

And get this, he's always going around saying how he doesn't know anything. "I know that I know nothing," he says. What kind of sense does that make? If you know you know nothing, you gotta know something, folks. I don't know about you, but I don't want a leader who doesn't know anything. That's how you end up with someone like Sleepy Joe. He doesn't know a single thing, but he somehow knows how to steal an election. We need someone who knows everything, like me!

And what's with the way he talks? He's always using these big words that nobody understands. I mean, come on, Socrates, speak English! I don't think he even knows what half of those words mean. He's just trying to sound smart. And believe me—I understand those words. I do. I have the best words. You might be asking yourself, "why doesn't he tell us what those big words mean?" Well, to be honest, folks, you really aren't missing much.

But here's the worst part. Socrates was always questioning authority, always questioning the government. That's not how things work, okay? You can't just go around questioning everything. You need to trust the experts, trust the people in charge. And Socrates, he was all about undermining the system. We need law and order in this country, law and order. Ancient Greece should have looked at what America was doing at the time; they would've seen guys like George Washington making sure that everyone was obeying the law.

So yeah, that's Socrates for you. A big talker, but no substance. A guy who thinks he's smart, but doesn't know anything. And a troublemaker who questions authority. Not the kind of guy you want running your city, believe me.

Democritus

Folks, have you heard of this guy Democritus? Let me tell you, he's got some wild ideas. I mean, he thinks that everything is made up of these tiny, invisible particles called atoms. Can you believe that? It sounds like something out of a sci-fi movie, doesn't it? A WOKE sci-fi movie no doubt! But this guy Democritus was serious about it. And get this, he also believed that the soul is made of atoms too. I mean, how ridiculous is that? Absolutely crazy, and absolutely crooked— terrible! It's no wonder that the Radical Left Do Noting Democrats named themselves after him! They just want to deny the truth of what we're made of— America!

Now, I'm all for thinking outside the box, but these ideas are just way too out there. He sounds like Crazy Bernie. I mean, how can we trust what we can't even see? To be totally honest with you, I think he's trying to pull a fast one on us. And get this, he also believed in an infinite number of worlds. Seriously? I mean, come on, how many worlds do we need? One is enough for me! We've got plenty to worry about at home. Mexico, China, and all their friends on the Left. Maybe those infinite worlds are where they got those extra votes!

But that's not all, he also thought that the universe is unchanging and eternal. Really? Can you imagine? That means no growth, no progress. What kind of world would that be? I'm all about winning and making things better. If the world was unchanging, how do you explain all my great big, beautiful buildings?

I believe in hard work, success, and making America great again. Not these crazy ideas about atoms and infinite worlds. Democritus— or as I call him, DEMOCRATius— can shove it.

Plato

Let me tell you, Plato was a real loser. He's all about these forms that he thinks are more real than what we can actually see, and frankly, that's just not smart, folks. We've got to deal with the real world, not some imaginary world. That's where you get ideas like the Green New Deal. He thinks that everything we see in the world is just a copy of some perfect form that exists in another realm. I mean, come on, folks, that's just ridiculous! And let's be honest, there's no way there's a copy of me out there. That's why you need me to stick around! Then he's got this whole thing about philosopher-kings. He thinks that only philosophers should be in charge of government. I know how to get things done as a businessman, and these philosophers couldn't run a business if their lives depended on it; they're too busy sitting around thinking! Now, if someone comes in and becomes a philosopher, now that could work. I think of myself as our first philosopher-president!

He just goes on and on about how we need to use reason instead of our emotions. It reminds me of a great philosopher of our time, he says something about how facts don't care about your feelings. But you know what? Emotions are important, folks! They're what make us winners and losers. I mean, can you imagine a world where nobody ever got angry or sad or happy? That would be a pretty boring world if you ask me. You could never tell when someone wasn't cut out for a job— like many people in charge are!

Plato's ultimately a loser. He's all about these fake ideas and fake news, and he thinks that philosophers should run the show. That's just not how the world works. We need people who know how to get things done, not people who spend all day thinking. When you think too much, you never get any action, and without action, how else are you supposed to be a winner?

Aristotle

I know a lot about Aristotle. He's a great guy, really, tremendous. He was a philosopher, but not as good as me. I mean, he's been dead for thousands of years, and I'm still alive and kicking. Joe even remembers meeting him! But I'll tell you what, he had some good ideas. Aristotle believed in this thing called logic. It's like when you have a really good argument and you use reason and facts to prove your point. And let me tell you, I'm the best at that. I've got the best logic, the best arguments, and nobody does it better than me. Did you see me in the debates against Crooked Hillary? Aristotle would have been proud.

He's got this virtue ethics or whatever; it's basically when you do the right thing because it's the right thing to do, instead of doing it because you want something out of it. Honestly, that's good. We should always try to do the right thing, especially if nobody's watching. Just look at me! I'm always trying to set the best example behind closed doors.

Now let's talk politics. He thought that the best form of government was a monarchy. It's a little concerning, but he's got a point! I mean, I'm the President, and I can't do anything I like. I still have to follow our great big beautiful Constitution. Wonderful document, let me tell you. Read it myself. And I've done a great job as President. Nobody can deny that. But folks, imagine how much more winning we could've had if it wasn't for Nancy Pelosi and Congress getting in the way! Aristotle would've understood, and he would've been MAGA all the way!

Mencius

Look folks, about this guy Mencius. Some people, and I won't name names— but if I did, let's just say it would rhyme with Creepy Moe— say he's not as great as Confucius. But let me tell you, I think Mencius has a lot of potential. He's a good guy, really smart, maybe even the best. Some people might say he's not as popular, but that's fake news, okay? He's very popular, believe me. He was way up in the polls.

Mencius believed in the importance of education and self-cultivation. And you know what, I agree with him. Education is so important, that's why I took the SAT all by myself, and I went to Wharton, which believe me, was the best institution until they started talking about CRT and all that. And self-cultivation? Well, those people in the lame-stream media are always saying I've got a cult-like following, which is pretty much what Mencius was talking about, and I think that's what he would have wanted. Now, Mencius also thought human nature was fundamentally good, and I gotta tell you, I like that. I mean, sure, some people are bad—and it's our job to weed out all the bad ones, but to be honest with you they make it pretty easy because they all call themselves Democrats— but deep down, I think everyone's got some goodness in them. And that's a beautiful thing, folks. We need more positivity like that. I do my best to put out nothing but positivity.

Those same not-so-smart people might say Mencius was too idealistic, that he didn't understand the world's harsh realities. But I think he was just a visionary. And that's what we need more of, folks. Big dreams, big visions, and the courage to pursue them. You know, I always said if you're gonna dream, dream big. Don't just build a fence, build a wall. Don't just be a president, be the only president. I think Mencius was a really great guy. Maybe not as well-known as some others, but that doesn't mean he's not important. After all, my favorite president, Andrew Jackson, no one has ever heard of him, and when people do talk about him, they say some things that are, quite frankly, very nasty and very unfair. I think we could all learn a thing or two from him. Thank you, Mencius, and thank you, China.

Zhuangzi

Folks, I gotta tell you, I just read this book by Zhuangzi. It's a Chinese book, and let me tell you, it's a great book. It's tremendous. A little hard to read sometimes, though. I had to find an English version about halfway through. I don't know if you've heard of it, but it's called the "Zhuangzi," and it's about this guy named Zhuangzi who has all these crazy ideas. I really like that naming idea. My next memoir is going to be called "The Donald."

He had this story about a guy dreaming he was a butterfly, but when he woke up, he wasn't sure if he was a man dreaming about being a butterfly, or a butterfly dreaming about being a man. That's a pretty deep thought, and it's very true of our world today! They say that I'm not the president anymore, but in a rightful world without the rigging, you'd have four more years! It's all about perspective, folks. It's like, who are we really? Are we who we think we are, or are we something else entirely? I don't know, folks, but it's a great question, and I'd expect that Zhuangzi would have some answers for us if he were still around; in fact, he probably could've clarified this whole election thing.

Something I really want you to understand is that, yes, Zhuangzi was a philosopher, but he wasn't like those boring old guys. He was actually—many people say this about me, too— a really funny guy. He thought we shouldn't take things too seriously, that we should just relax and go with the flow. I like that, I think that's a good idea. You know, I'm probably, maybe even the funniest president the country has had. The Democrats, they don't know what humor even is— except for when they ARE the joke, which is all the time!

Zhuangzi had some great one-liners, too, just unbelievable. He said things like, "Happiness is the absence of striving for happiness," and "The wise find pleasure in water; the virtuous find pleasure in hills. The wise are active and joyful, and the virtuous are tranquil and long-lived." I don't know what half of that means, but it sounds really smart. The wise men— like me and a lot of other very smart people like me— are active, which means we're winners. The virtuous are tranquil, which means they're lazy! And you know who is lazy and long-lived? That's right! Sleepy Joe! If you're virtuous like Zhuangzi says, you're never gonna succeed. Sad!

Some of those very sleepy and frankly, very weak people might say that Zhuangzi's ideas are too out there. And you know, China might be far away, but it's not that far. And I think he's onto something. We need to start having fun with things. And you know what the best way to have fun is? That's right, folks. You gotta win at those things. No one has ever been a loser and said they had fun. That's why I make them so angry. They gotta loosen up!

Pyrrhon of Elis

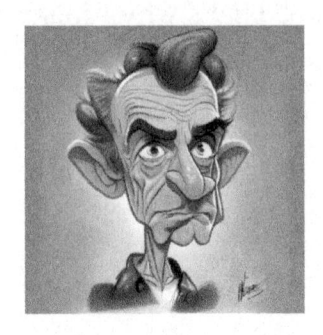

Pyrrhon of Elis was from ancient Greece, which is apparently where all the really important people are from. But, personally, I'm not so sure he's all that important. You know me, I'm a big believer in facts and the truth, especially when it's on my side, and sometimes you even need some alternative facts! Pyrrhon was all about doubt and questioning everything. Sounds a lot like that guy Socrates, folks, and that does not bode well, let me tell you.

He was all about suspending judgment and not making conclusions. He was always questioning everything. It's like he couldn't make up his mind about anything. We should call him Pick-a-side Pyrrhon! Some people might say that's a good thing. But let me tell you, skepticism can be a real problem, folks, because it gets in the way of progress. You have to take risks and trust your instincts. That's how you get ahead in life. Otherwise, you're just a loser like the rest of 'em. And you know, some people might say that Pyrrhon was just being cautious. That he wanted to make sure he knew what he was talking about before he made any big claims. But you can't just sit around doubting everything all the time. If you do that, you become, and I hate to say it, really low energy and really uninteresting. That's right, folks— you become Jeb Bush.

And get a load of this, he wasn't even sure about his own senses! Well, I don't know about you, but I trust my senses. I trust what I see, what I hear. Pick-a-side Pyrrhon couldn't even trust himself. That's how you can tell a real loser! So, Pyrrhon, he really isn't worth talking about. I'm not so sure about this whole skepticism thing— it makes, me, frankly, kind of skeptical. You can't win that way, folks. Trust me.

Epicurus

Listen folks, some people say Epicurus was a philosopher, some people say he was a hedonist, but let me tell you, nobody knows for sure. I think that there's not much of a difference between the two. Not that we can even really know. I mean, the guy lived over 2,000 years ago, who really knows what he was all about? He didn't even write it down in English!

Epicurus believed in living a simple life. And come on; who wants to live like that? I have a beautiful wife— just talk to any of them, they're just terrific, highest paid women in America— and beautiful kids, and beautiful things all around me. But Epicurus didn't believe in any of that. He thought that people should live without pain, and that they should only seek pleasure that doesn't lead to pain in the long run. I mean, what kind of philosophy is that? Some of the greatest things in this country's history wouldn't have happened if we listened to Scaredy-cat Epicurus! It was a great pleasure to be your president, and we all felt the pain of it being stolen from us. But did that make it not worth it? No! Now some people might think that I have a lot in common with Epicurus because of his views on pleasure. But let me tell you, nobody likes pleasure more than me, okay? I mean, have you seen my apartment? And I've got the best resorts, the best golf courses. Just look at Mar-a-Lago. You know what they call it?

They say it's like the White House of the South, folks, and that's gotta be positive. But let me tell you, there's a difference between the way I enjoy life and the way Epicurus did it. See, I understood that pleasure, when you really get down to it, comes from being rich. Just look at all the losers who are miserable all the time!

Get this— Epicurus believed in something called the "atomism" theory. He thought everything in the universe was made up of tiny pieces called atoms. Can you believe that? I mean, what is he even talking about? You think I'm made of the same stuff as Crooked Hillary and Sleepy Joe? What a racket! But I'll tell you what, I do agree with him on one thing. He said that we should live in the moment. And that's exactly what I do. And that's what you should all do too. Don't worry about these philosophers and their crazy ideas. Just live your life because that's how we're going to make America great again.

Zeno of Citium

Folks, let me tell you about Zeno of Citium, one of the great philosophers of ancient Greece. Now, some people might say he was the founder of the Stoic school of philosophy, but I like to think of him as a true winner. Because that's what we're all about, folks: winning. Zeno thought a lot about virtue. And I'm the most virtuous person you'll ever meet. I've got more integrity than anyone else. I mean, just look at all the great things I've done for this country. No one else could have done what I've done, folks. But we're not talking about Zhuangzi's virtue, okay? Zeno's virtue means reason, and reason means results!

Zeno had this idea of not giving in to desire. When we let our desires control us, we can make bad decisions. And I never make bad decisions, folks. I always make the best decisions. Believe me. When I make a decision, all the winners around me say it was just the best. But the not-so-great people, the disloyal sleaze bags, they run to the media. Truly pathetic! Zeno would never do that, I think.

Now, Zeno thought we should try to find harmony with nature, and that we shouldn't get too tied up in passion and emotion. That sounds good to me, folks, but let me tell you, we can still have passion and emotion and win bigly. Look at me, I'm one of the most passionate people you'll ever meet, and I've won more than anyone else. And as for the harmony with nature, you gotta understand that nature is what America is all about! The more land we have, the more this great big, beautiful country can stretch across the world!

So, Zeno was a great guy, a really smart guy. But you know what, folks? He didn't have what it takes to be a winner like me. Because at the end of the day, it's not just about being reasonable and virtuous. It's about winning. And no one wins like me, folks. Believe me. I'm a businessman, and I know how important it is to make decisions. I called him a winner, but the truth is, he's just a lousy fake like so many others. But hey, that's life when you're surrounded by so many smart people. Some of them are going to turn out to be not-so-smart.

Philo of Judaeus

Philo of Judea? I'm telling you folks; nobody knew more about Judaism than me. I mean, I've got Jews in my family, okay? I let my daughter marry one of them! I've been to Israel, and they are just the best people, really. Their neighbors, not so much, but that's why we have to keep helping them out. So let me tell you about this guy, Philo. Some people say he was a philosopher, but I don't know folks, I think he was more like the lame-stream media. You know, he was the kind of guy who makes you believe whatever he wants. Makes you think about who's in charge of all of that!

And you know, Philo was around back when the world was simpler. But let me tell you, he didn't make things any simpler. He was always going on about these allegories and symbols, like he was trying to hide something. And don't even get me started on his ideas about God. He thought God was this perfect being, not involved in the world at all. But I've always said, I like a God who's involved in things, who's making deals and getting things done, you know what I mean? If God wasn't down here in the world, then how else would he be an American, huh? Even Jesus— a very famous Jew and a very famous American— understood that!

Plus, there's his views on the afterlife, thinking the soul is immortal, which is just crazy. I mean, nobody knows what happens when we die. You want someone to tell you what happens after we die? Go ask weak and cowardly Mike Pence! But this guy, Shifty Philo, he thought he had all the answers. He was always trying to merge Judaism with Greek ideas. But really, folks, you know it and I know it; we should all just stick to our own traditions. We don't need to borrow from the Greeks. They've got their own problems to deal with. The best thing about America is our refusal to learn from other countries. After all, what do they do that we don't do better?

Sneaky Philo, he was a smart guy, I'll give him that, but he was smart like a politician is smart (which is not very smart at all), always trying to spin things, and while we don't know this for sure, probably did some things for some money, too. And as far as I'm concerned, that's not what's going to make America great again, folks.

Epictetus

So, Epictetus is not the most famous philosopher, but he's still pretty good. Didn't poll super highly, would've dropped out before whatever the Greek version of Iowa is. You know, he's from ancient Greece, just like those other guys I've talked about before. But this guy, he's different. He's all about stoicism, about being tough, being resilient, and not letting anything get to you. Just like me, right? Nothing ever bothers me!

Epictetus said that we should always try to be better people. That's a good message, right? Maybe this guy would've polled a little bit better than I thought. I mean, I'm always trying to improve myself. That's why I'm so successful. I'm a winner, and I'm always looking for ways to be an even bigger winner. He seems like a winner, too. Vice presidential material maybe. But what really sets Epictetus apart is his focus on personal responsibility. He believed that we're in control of our own happiness and that we shouldn't blame others for our problems. Now, that's something I can get behind. I mean, sure, the fake news media and those radical leftists are always trying to bring me down, but I don't let them get to me. I'm in control of my own destiny, just like Epictetus. Never bothered me one bit. Also, I like that idea of never blaming anyone. It's always our fault. For example, the Obama administration should've recognized it was their fault for letting China and Mexico ruin our economy! Sad and weak!

Now, Epictetus had some pretty radical ideas. He believed that people shouldn't get too attached to material things, you know, like money or fancy cars. Now, I understand that, but I'd imagine that was a lot easier back when they hadn't invented fancy cars yet. But still, there's something to be said for not getting too caught up in material possessions. I mean, just look at those Democrats and their obsession with big government and socialist policies. That's not stoic at all! They're always crying and whining about how much winning we're doing! It's not stoic to hate America, folk, not stoic at all. But I sorta get it, because this guy Epictetus, he was born a slave, which in those times, you really didn't want to be. But he didn't let that get to him. He said something like, "I may be a slave, but I can still control my mind." That's stoicism for you. Even after he became free and came up with all this smart stuff, he never forgot where he came from. That's something I can appreciate. He never even asked for any reparations or anything! Maybe those Democrats should take a page out of his book. But they won't!

Marcus Aurelius

Marcus Aurelius? Terrible leader, just terrible. Have you seen the movie *Gladiator*? He gets killed fifteen minutes in by that scrawny guy! He had this thing called Stoicism, and let me tell you, it's not good. He's like, "Oh, don't let your emotions control you, focus on what you can control," blah, blah, blah. But what about feelings, folks? What about being passionate? You need to be passionate, you need to have emotions, otherwise you're just a robot. I'd like to say, and I'd like to think, that I'm a pretty passionate guy. I'm passionate about this country and passionate about all of you beautiful people. You know what you become when you're not passionate! Sleepy and low energy!

And he was all about this "virtue" thing, which is just another way of saying "good behavior." Well, I'm sorry, but I'm a winner, folks. And sometimes you gotta do what you gotta do to win. It's not about being virtuous, it's about being successful. Mini Marcus just didn't understand, and that's why Rome didn't do too well after he died.

Plus, he was way too focused on death. Always talking about death, death, death. But I'm sorry, I plan on living forever. I have the best genes, believe me. And if I do die, it's gonna be the greatest death in history. Everyone will remember it, it'll be huge. Have you seen the funerals for some other presidents? It's gonna blow those out of the water, folks.

So no, I'm not a fan of Miserable Marcus Aurelius. He was weak, he was boring, and frankly, he just didn't have what it takes to be a great leader like me.

Nagarjuna

Alright, folks, let me tell you about this guy Nagarjuna, who some people say is one of the most important philosophers in Buddhism. But first, let me tell you, folks, you should never touch that stuff. It ruins lives. Just say no, kids. But this guy, he's no match for me! I mean, have you seen the size of my crowds? Huge!

So Nagarjuna was all about this idea called "emptiness." Sounds pretty depressing, right? But don't worry, I'm sure he had some great ideas in there somewhere. Anyway, he believed that everything in the world is empty of inherent existence. Sorry, Nagarjuna, but that just sounds like a bunch of mumbo-jumbos to me. See what kind of nonsense you come up with when your brain is on that stuff, folks?

Get this, he also believed that the Buddha himself was empty! Can you believe it? This guy was talking smack about the Buddha! And let me tell you, nobody disrespects a religious figure on my watch. Not even me! In Trump Tower, I've got pictures of all the great religious figures; Jesus, Muhammad, all of them.

It gets even crazier! Nagarjuna also said that the concept of karma is empty! Can you believe it? No karma? That means nobody gets what's coming to them, no matter how many times they cheat on their taxes or refuse to release their tax returns. I'm not sure I'm on board with this one, folks. Doesn't sound a whole lot like draining the swamp to me. But don't worry, even though Nagarjuna was all about emptiness, he still believed in the importance of compassion. Sounds nice, right? I guess he was trying to make up for all the crazy stuff he was saying about the Buddha and karma. But let me tell you, nobody's more compassionate than me. I love all Americans, especially the ones who voted for me. Nagarjuna may have been a big deal in Buddhism, but he's got nothing on me. My ideas are the best ideas, believe me. And remember kids, that stuff will ruin lives!

Plotinus

So, this guy, Plotinus— I mean, what kind of name is Plotinus? It sounds like a combination of a vegetable and a body part. But anyway, he's supposed to be some big deal philosopher who lived a long time ago. I didn't realize vegetables could be philosophers. I thought they were just science guys! So, Plotinus believed in something called Neoplatonism, which honestly folks, is not a word. I don't know who thought it was a good idea to write that down, but it's not a real word. I'd know, I know all the words. The first book I ever read was the dictionary, and as we all know, there aren't any new words, so I'd say I'm a pretty good authority on the subject. I don't know about you, but I like my philosophy like I like my steaks— well-done, straightforward, and plain. Maybe some ketchup, too. But Neoplatonism is all about the soul and how to become one with the universe. Sounds like a bunch of hippie nonsense to me. You'd need some Nagarjuna to understand it!

Plotinus believed that there were three stages of soul development. First, you've got the sensory stage, where you only care about yourself. Then you move on to the reason stage, where you start to think outside of your world a little bit. Maybe care about others. I think a lot of decent people are in this stage. And finally, you reach the divine stage, where you become one with the universe. Pretty freaky. I don't know about you, but I think I'm already at the third stage. What could be better than being a billionaire and President of the United States? That's pretty divine if you ask me. The other presidents, they weren't in *Home Alone 2*. Sad and undivine!

Anyway, Plotinus believed that we could achieve this divine state by contemplating the divine, which he called the One. But get this, he also believed that the One was beyond all human understanding. So how are we supposed to contemplate something that we can't even understand? It's like reading a book in Chinese or Spanish or something, and trust me, I've tried but it doesn't make any sense. Which One, Plotinus? Which One are you talking about? And to make things worse, he's got this thing called emanation, where the whole universe comes from the One. So basically, everything is just a worse version of the divine. I don't know about you, but I like when my things are original, not some cheap knock-off. That's what happens when we import everything from China, and that's why it's so important to bring back our manufacturing jobs. You know where the One might be? Ohio! Plotinus seems to think that we can become one with the universe by contemplating something we can't understand, and that everything is just a cheap imitation of the divine. Sounds like a bunch of bull to me. But what do I know, I'm just a billionaire president! It's not like I'd know anything about winning in this universe!

Sextus Empiricus

Let me tell you something about this guy, Sextus Empiricus, okay? Frankly, I'm not really impressed. Kind of low energy. Funny name though. First of all, he was a skeptic. And we've talked already about how ridiculous that is! Now I love being critical, but this guy? He took it to a whole new level. He doubted everything, even doubted his own existence! Can you believe that? How can you be a philosopher if you doubt your own existence? More importantly, how can you be a winner?

Get this: he thought that there's no such thing as objective truth. Everything depends on your point of view, which is just insane! I mean, how can we know anything then? How can we make decisions? This is what the radical woke left wants us to believe. It's all about "my truth" and "my experience." Well let me tell you, there's a lot of nasty people out there who will make up nasty things— and even sue you for it! This is why objective truth is so important, and that's why it's so great that it perfectly aligns with me. But the worst thing about Shifty Sextus, the thing that really gets to me, is that he thinks we should give up on judging everything. Everything! He didn't want us to make any decisions or take any actions, which is really the mark of a true loser. That's not philosophy, that's laziness. It's like he wants us to live in a world of inaction and apathy. And let me tell you folks, if there are two things that I really care about, it's action and pathy. That's the path to making America great, folks.

Saint Augustine

Let me tell you, folks, Saint Augustine was a big deal. Huge. He was a philosopher, theologian, and bishop; all of them! Let me tell you, he was one of the best. He wrote about so many different things, and he did it so well you wouldn't believe it. Like this tell-all book *Confessions*! And then there's *City of God*, which is sort of like a guide to running basically a perfect city. If you want to make your city great again, you need to read that book. It's a bestseller, trust me. Almost as good as *The Art of the Deal*. Sadly, it looks like the Democrats aren't reading it, because our inner cities are just a mess. Just a mess. If Saint Augustine could see them today, he'd be shocked. Then again, he'd probably be shocked by things like cars and cell phones, too.

And you know, Saint Augustine wasn't afraid to ask the tough questions. And folks, I'm about that too. In business, you ask the tough questions that everyone else is too scared to ask, and you don't stop until you get the answers you want. That's how to be a winner, folks. And let me tell you, that was Saint Augustine. He became a bishop, which is like the ultimate winner back then. Who's a better judge of winning than God, am I right?

You know what's really impressive? He was born in Africa, and he became one of the most important thinkers in the West. That's a huge accomplishment, folks. I mean, I was born to a working-class family in Queens, and with just a small loan of a million dollars, I built a company that made me President of the United States, so I know a thing or two about breaking barriers. Not only that, but I was also the first guy to defeat a woman in the presidential election! Talk about shattering the glass ceiling! But you know, Saint Augustine was next level, truly one of the greatest African American thinkers of our time. I think if he were alive today, he'd really help me get the black vote. If you're looking for someone to inspire you to be a winner, Real-Deal Saint Augustine is your guy. You won't be disappointed. If you don't trust God, then trust me!

Hypatia

I know all about Hypatia. She was a philosopher, a mathematician, and an astronomer. A real smart gal. Now, the main thing you need to know about Hypatia, the most important thing about her, is that she was a woman. And I love women, believe me, nobody loves women more than me. I love women so much I got married three times, folks. That's a presidential record. No one is as good at women as I am. But at the end of the day, folks, there's just not much Hypatia could do. She just came off— and I mean this in the nicest way possible— a little bit nasty. She didn't know how to make people like her. She needed someone to show her how to survive, show her the ropes, negotiate with people. It's really unfortunate that she just had to go and die instead. I think she would've made a lovely running mate had she just listened to me.

But what they don't tell you about Hypatia is that she was a total disaster. She was a loser, folks, a stone-cold woman loser. She may have been smart, but her deal-making skills weren't quite there. A little too emotional. She couldn't negotiate her way through a McDonald's order. And you know what happened in the end? A mob killed her. That's right, a mob. She just couldn't get the people to love her— like I said, a bit of a nasty woman sometimes. Very abrasive. Very hard to work with. Not obedient. I've seen what mobs can do, and yes, sometimes they can get a little bit excited, and sometimes in that excitement they can storm the Capitol, but the truth is that they're just very passionate people! Hypatia just didn't have that passion, and that's why she lost.

You know what else they don't tell you about her? You'd think she's a good Christian lady, but no, she was a pagan. And you know how I feel about those types of people, folks. I don't like 'em one bit. I mean, what kind of philosophy is that? It doesn't make any sense; they're just worshiping a bunch of statues! What a terrible way to try to live your life. The only statues we need are the Lincoln Memorial and Jesus! Hysterical "Rosie O'Donnell" Hypatia may have been smart, but she was a total failure, a total disaster. She got nothing done, she didn't know how to work with people— men or women, and she was all around just a very unpleasant woman to work with. I mean, what more is there to say? She's a nobody, a total loser, and frankly, probably not very attractive.

Sankara

Hey, folks. Today we're going to talk about Sankara. He was a philosopher from India, which, by the way, is one of my favorite countries. I mean, I love India. I have lots of friends there, great people. Great food, too. I even have a Trump Tower in Mumbai. It's huge!

So, Sankara was a big deal in India, like a really big deal. He was all about this thing called Advaita Vedanta, which is like this crazy philosophy that says everything is just one thing, and that one thing is Brahman. And let me tell you, Brahman is a really great thing. Believe me, folks, it's the best thing. My favorite superhero. I loved Michael Keaton, but not so much Ben Affleck. Total liberal and not very smart. Sad and hates guns! Melania is much more attractive than J-Lo!

Now, some people think that Sankara was just a big ol' smarty-pants who loved to argue with people. But you know what? I kind of like that about him. I mean, I love to argue with people too. It's one of my favorite things to do. And let me tell you, folks, nobody argues like I do. I have the best arguments, the most beautiful arguments you've ever seen. I don't get in a lot of arguments over there in India, though. I have great relations with the Indian people. Wonderful people. I don't know why the British let them go. I would've worked out a better deal.

Anyway, back to Sankara. He had this idea that the world we see is just an illusion, and that the only real thing is Brahman. And you know what? I kind of get where he's coming from. I mean, have you seen some of the things people are saying about me in the fake news? It's like they're living in a different reality. But let me tell you, folks, the real reality is that I'm the best president this country has ever had. The lame-stream media might keep telling the liberal coastal elites what they want to hear, but it's just an illusion. They don't know what's going on in this country. Brahman would be a real American!

But getting back to Sankara, he was all about meditation and stuff like that. And you know what? I think meditation is great. I mean, I don't really do it myself, because I'm always too busy making America great again. But I've heard it's very relaxing. Maybe I should try it sometime. I bet I'd be the best meditator ever. Nobody would meditate like I do. We offer the best meditations at Trump Tower in our spas. They're the best. Lots of Indians or whatever who work there.

Anyway, Sankara was a really smart guy, and he had a big influence on Indian philosophy. I mean, when I went to India, it reminded me a lot of America, and I really think it would be a great 51st state. And you know what? I bet if Sankara were alive today, he'd love America too. Because you know what America is all about? Winning. And nobody wins like I do, folks. Nobody. And Sankara understood that.

Trumping Philosophy | 56

So, there you have it, folks. Sankara was a great philosopher, and I'm a great president. It's just like Sankara said: everything is one thing, and that one thing is winning!

Al-Farabi

Oh boy, Al-Farabi! Now, that's a name you don't hear every day, folks. Kind of a weird name, kind of a scary name. Sounds a lot like some very nasty people abroad—I'm not gonna name names, and it's not because I can't spell them. But let me tell you, Al-Farabi was a big deal. He was a philosopher, a musician, a scientist - the guy did it all. And let me tell you, nobody does it better than Al-Farabi.

Now, some people might say, "Oh, Al-Farabi, he's just another philosopher from the Middle East." But let me tell you, he was much more than that. He was a genius, a real mastermind, which is really interesting when you think about how all he had to work with was a lot of sand and oil. He was so smart, in fact, that he wrote a book about how to be a good ruler. And let me tell you, nobody knows more about being a good ruler than me. I think Al-Farabi would've learned a lot from me. I could've helped write that book. An English version at least.

But back to Al-Farabi. He was a big believer in the power of music. He thought that music could have a huge impact on people's emotions and even their behavior. And you know what? I agree with him. That's why I always play "Macho Man"

Trumping Philosophy | 58

by the Village People at my rallies. Gets everybody pumped up and ready to win. I don't know what they listen to over there, but I'm sure whatever flutes or snake charmers he had were great musicians. I bet his rallies were a real show. So much so that they still love rallying in the Middle East, although they look considerably angrier now.

But let's not forget Al-Farabi's contributions to science. He was an expert in astronomy and mathematics. And you know what? I love math. In fact, I'm very good at math. Some people say I'm the best at math. Because you know what math is? It's business. The business of numbers. And what is an equation? It's making a deal between two sides.

Now, I know some people might be thinking, "Donald, what do you know about Al-Farabi? You don't even read books." Well, let me tell you, I don't need to read books to know about Al-Farabi. People tell me about him all the time. And you know what? When I understand them, they say he was a great guy. A real winner. I think I met him once on one of my trips over there.

So, in conclusion, folks, Al-Farabi was a brilliant philosopher, musician, and scientist. He knew how to be a good ruler, he loved music, and he was a math genius. And you know what? I think he would have been a big fan of mine, and that might be the smartest thing about him above all.

Avicenna

Avicenna, folks, was an Islamic philosopher and scientist from the medieval era. Tremendous guy, believe me. People are saying he was one of the greatest thinkers of all time, and you know what, they're right. Avicenna was really into what's called "metaphysics." Big word, but basically it means he was interested in figuring out what makes the universe tick. It's sort of like all the stuff in physics that you don't see. Like gravity. And space. Let me tell you, he had some great ideas. He believed that there's this thing called the "necessary being" which is basically the cause of everything else in the universe. Very deep stuff. It's sort of like Jesus, but for other people!

Guess what, folks? Avicenna was a really smart doctor, let me tell you. If I were his patient, he'd give me a clean bill of health! Mental and physical! He wrote this book— the *Canon of Medicine*, really just the best. It was like the medical bible for centuries. Seriously, folks, they loved him so much that they let a Muslim write a Bible! Goes to show that maybe we're not so different after all. Maybe they can use it to figure out the problem with Sleepy Joe! He's sure got some of those people in his White House!

He wasn't just a philosopher and a doctor though, folks. He was a damn good politician, advising all kinds of rulers. And you know what? They listened to him. He was that smart. A much better advisor than some of these RINOs I had to deal with. He believed that the ideal government was one that was ruled by a wise philosopher-king. And you know what, I gotta say, I agree with him on that one. We need more smart people in government, believe me. Nowadays we might be best off with a president-king!

Now, some people—and honestly, they aren't that smart— say that Avicenna was too focused on logic and reason. They say he didn't pay enough attention to emotions and feelings. But you know what, folks? I think he had it right. You can't just go around doing whatever feels good. You gotta use your brain. That's what separates us from the animals and the Democrats, and that's what's important!

Ramanuja

Well folks, today we're talking about Ramanuja, and I don't know why someone would name their child after a brand of cheap noodles, but hey, I guess they do it a little bit differently in other countries. He's from India, and let me tell you, he's a real thinker. He had a lot of ideas that were apparently so good that people are still talking about him today. Some of those people— and I'm not sure if they're really the smartest people, we'll have to see— call him a "philosopher saint." Now, I don't know how Ramanuja felt about that title, but I know a thing or two about that position. I had to be a stable genius businessman and the President at the same time— they call me "businessman president," or maybe "president businessman." I'm not sure, we're still workshopping the name.

But this story goes all the way back to 1017, a long time ago, folks, in South India. Ramanuja studied at a young age to become a priest, which is really interesting because I didn't know they had churches in that area back then. But then he got into philosophy and started asking a lot of questions, which I gotta tell you, must have been a real pain for his parents when he was that young. He was really into this idea of "bhakti," which is basically devotion to God. And let me tell you, nobody's more devoted to God than me, folks. I mean, have you seen the Trump Tower? That's a temple right there. The inside plated in gold? Practically a Synagogue.

But unlike some of these other weak and spineless philosophers who were all about sacrifice, Ramanuja had the much more reasonable idea that you didn't need to give up your body to be close to God. Some say you need to live in a cave or whatever in order to do that, but not Ramanuja. He thought you could do it by doing good things in the world. And just look at all the good stuff we've done for this country, incredible, really. I think Jesus would be MAGA if he was looking down on where this country is at. But Ramanuja also had this idea that God was in everything. That's pretty deep, if you think about it. He thought that God was in nature— the rocks and the animals and all that. And you know what, folks? I think he's right. I mean, have you seen a bald eagle? That's God's bird right there. Now, some people say that Ramanuja was all about escaping from the world and getting closer to God. But I don't think that's true, folks. I think he was all about being in the world and making it a better place. And you know what? That's the kind of Make America Great Again attitude I like to see in philosophers, folks. He got it.

Solomon Ibn Gabirol

So, Solomon ibn Gabirol, huh? First of all, what kind of name is that? Sounds like something out of Star Wars. I mean, I know I've got a weird name too, but at least it's memorable, right? Anyway, Ibn Gabirol was this Jewish philosopher from Spain back in the 11th century. Now, I know what you're thinking - how can a Jewish guy from Spain be a philosopher? I've spent a lot of time at Synagogues, folks, and I've never seen any Mexicans there, much less any of them thinking about the world— or excuse me, "el mundo." But trust me, folks, it's true. Some people also call him Solomon Ben Judah, which I think makes a lot more sense— then we can just call him Ben— but it doesn't quite sound as cool, now does it? So ultimately, he had to go with the pick that was a little less kosher.

Ibn Gabirol was another one of these guys really into this thing called Neoplatonism. Now, I do like that ice cream flavor, believe me, we serve it at Trump Tower's café, but here we're talking about how one big God who created everything, but then also created all these little beings to help him out. And you know what, that makes a lot of sense for a Spanish guy.

Ibn Gabirol also talked a lot about the nature of existence and reality. And let me tell you, folks, I know all about that. I'm a bit of an expert on reality. I've had the greatest reality TV show ever. It's been so great. But you know the thing they don't tell you about reality TV? Its nature isn't always what you see. We can change things around, especially when we need to show how weak and loser-like someone is. I can change the reality, so I really know what Ibn Gabriol was talking about, believe me.

But you know what really impressed me about Ibn Gabirol? There's this book he wrote, *The Fount of Life,* which is all about how the universe is made up of ten different "intellectual virtues." Now, I don't know what all those words mean, but I do know that ten is a great number. It's like how I've got ten billion dollars. Okay, maybe not ten billion, but it's a lot, believe me. Now if each of those billions of dollars was a virtue, Ibn Gabirol would be proud!

Al-Ghazali

Nobody knows what Al-Ghazali is talking about; it's really ridiculous, and frankly, it's kind of embarrassing for him. He's always going on and on about how he's some kind of holy man or something, but nobody knows what he actually believes. Big loser energy, really. One day he'll say one thing, and the next day he'll say the exact opposite. He can't make up his mind about anything. Al-Ghazali? They shoulda called him Al-Gha-phony! What's with all these guys named Al, anyway?

And don't even get me started on his writing style. I mean, what is with all these fake words? It's like he's trying to sound smarter than he actually is. It's just a bunch of gibberish if you ask me. But you know what's really funny? This guy is always going on about how we can't trust our senses or our reason. But then, he'll totally change his tune as soon as it's convenient! A real two-face, folks, that's for sure. He'll turn around and say something like "Allah exists and is the only reality." It's like he thinks we can't hear! I mean, didn't you just say we can't know anything for sure? That seems a little bit like he's leading you on, folks. I know bull better than anyone else, and it seems like he's full of it. The best part is—what he's sure about is the part that's most obviously fake! I mean, it's like he's trying to have it both ways. He wants to be this deep thinker, but he's not really saying anything. And let's not forget, this guy spent his whole life studying the Quran and Islamic theology, which honestly? That really just discredits him. You'd think he'd be sure of at least his bad taste in books. And you know what they say about theologians, right? They're just making stuff up as they go along. I mean, we all know there's only one prophet—Jesus— because he's the American prophet!

Al-Ghazali talks a lot but doesn't really say anything. He's always changing his mind and nobody knows what he actually believes. And let's be honest, his writing is a snooze fest. Stick to the real philosophers, folks. You're not missing much with this one— and frankly, he doesn't seem to be missing much by not being sure of his own beliefs either.

Peter Abelard

Oh boy, let me tell you folks, we've got a real winner with Peter Abelard. He's one of the most famous philosophers of the medieval period, and let me tell you, he's got some serious ideas. Some of them are great, believe me, some of them are really fantastic, but some of them are just, well, let's just say they're not so great, but we'll handle that when we come to it. Abelard was all about reason, believing we should use our minds to figure out the truth instead of just accepting what we're being told by the mainstream media. And I love that. We need to be tougher on the information that's out there, because frankly, a lot of it is untrue, and more importantly, not very nice about me. Or you.

But then, Abelard goes and gets all weird about love. He's got this thing for Heloise, who was his student, and it's all very scandalous. I mean, look, I love beautiful women, who doesn't? Like I said, I've got the best beautiful women, and I've made two of the most beautiful women with those other beautiful women! But you've got to draw the line somewhere, folks— I'm not sure that dating your student is really the best idea. I know I've said some things about my daughter before, but really— a student! It's just shameful, and it goes to show

Trumping Philosophy | 68

you how much he couldn't get any women who were appropriate for him. Abelard just couldn't keep to himself.

And his ideas about religion— oh boy. Abelard was always getting into trouble with the Church, and I can relate to that. I mean, I've had my fair share of run-ins with those guys, especially in some of those southern states. But Abelard's solution was just to pick and choose different stories, which you just can't do folks. You can't just decide that you're only going to follow the parts of a religion that you like. That's not how it works. You gotta commit to it all, except for the parts you don't want to. You gotta listen to the denominations that do the picking for you. That's how a real winner does religion.

Averroes

Alright, let's talk about Averroes. A lot of people are saying he's a philosopher, a scholar, a judge, and all these things. But let me tell you, he's not that great, okay? He's overrated. First of all, he's from Spain. And what do they know about philosophy in Spain? Nothing. I mean, I know a lot of people from Spain, they're great people, but philosophy? Come on. You can't do philosophy in Spanish, everyone knows that! For construction, maybe, and sometimes for buying things in a bodega. Otherwise, it's just a total disaster.

And then he's all about this thing called Aristotelianism. You know, I thought at first that was a word in Spanish, and I swear I've heard those people say something like that over and over, but it turns out it just means that it's based on Aristotle, who was a great guy! It's kind of like how I've got Trumpism. Hey, maybe that'll become a philosophy one day.

There's this part of Aristotelianism called "double truths," which is a phrase I really like. He's basically saying that there are two truths, one for religion and one for philosophy. And I can see where he's coming from. It's kind of like alternative facts! And let's not forget about his criticism of Al-Gha-phony.

Trumping Philosophy | 70

It shows that Averroes really got it; sometimes you just gotta go on the attack.

So yeah, I actually think Averroes is definitely one of the good ones, and he'd be a great representative of the campaign to reach the Hispanic community if he were alive today.

Zhu-Xi

Zhu Xi? He was another Chinese one, and honestly, I wouldn't be so trusting of him if I were there back then. I know another Xi, and he's done nothing but rip us off! But this other guy Zhu Xi, he believed in something called neo-Confucianism. Now, I'm a fan of Confucius, but I don't know what The Matrix has to do with him. Maybe it just plays better in China. Anyways, this guy thought that you could achieve inner peace by studying the classics. What a loser! Trust me, folks, I've read plenty of the so-called "classics" like Jane Austen and Ernest Hemingway, and to be honest they were pretty boring. The only classic we need is the Declaration of Independence and our great big beautiful Constitution, with all of its words of freedom.

And get this: Zhu Xi thought that you had to understand the universe before you can understand yourself. That's like saying you have to understand the whole world to be successful in business. Wrong! You just need to know what's best for you. That's all that matters. If we were to understand everything that goes on out there, we'd never be able to learn a single thing about ourselves. After all, no one can understand what's going on in the minds of the Left! It would be hopeless! He also had this idea about two main forces called yin and yang.

Now, the yin part I'm not too sure about, but the yang part seems to have caught on, especially with how many of them there are! Every time I'm in a business meeting with China, it's always "Oh, Mr. President, let me introduce you to Mr. Yang." How many of these guys are there?

But luckily, he had a process, which is good. Always gotta have a process to things. Zhu Xi had these four stages of knowledge. First, you learn things. Then, you reflect on them. Then, you discuss them with others. And lastly, you achieve enlightenment. Now, I understand the appeal of each of those, but I what I don't quite get is why we need to discuss things with others before enlightenment. When I say something, I'm gonna say it right. So, I'm going to be enlightened before I discuss things with others, and then if they're right, too, I can tell how loyal those people are. Otherwise, what's the point?

The truth is, folks, Zhu Xi just didn't have what it took. He looked up to one of the great men from China, but he just fell short. Nowadays, he might have been MAGA on the surface, but a RINO at heart.

Maimonides

Well let me tell you, folks, we've got Maimonides. A very smart guy, very very smart. Some people say he's one of the greatest Jewish philosophers of all time. Tremendous. I've already made clear how much I love Jewish people, they're really terrific. And this guy, one of the best— and dare I say most— Jewish guys out there, a big fan of reason and logic. He wrote a lot about how to use your brain to understand God. I mean, I love that stuff, I really do. But some people say it's not enough, that you need faith too. But let me tell you, without reason, how can you even have faith? This is what I'm talking about, these people just have it all figured out.

But here's the thing about Maimonides. He was all about finding the middle ground, the balance between extremes. Now, I'm not too sure about that. If there's one side— me— and the other side— the Left— why would we need balance? Clearly one is better than the other! It feels a little skittish and weak, to be honest, and maybe— I don't know if this is entirely the case but it might be— a little more backbone would've helped these guys out in some sticky situations. Maimonides wouldn't want a balance between him and Hitler, right?

Maimonides also wrote a lot about the importance of charity and helping others, which is pretty surprising! And I'm all for that, folks. I mean, I'm very charitable, believe me. I give a lot of money to charity. That's how I've paid so little in taxes, I just give a lot away. You can see it on my returns.

Now, some people criticize Maimonides for not being religious enough, trying to rationalize everything. But you know what? I think he was just being honest. You can't make yourself believe something that doesn't make sense. That's how you become a Democrat! And that's what I like about Maimonides, he was honest. Maimonides was a very smart guy— very logical, very balanced. I like that. I really do. And let me tell you, we need more of that in this world.

Ibn Al-Arabi

Ibn al-Arabi— let me tell you, folks, this guy was a real thinker. Some people call him the "Greatest Master" and let me tell you, I know a thing or two about being a great master. But this guy was on another level. He was born in Spain in the 12th century, which is like, really old. It's so old that they had Muslim Mexicans back then— different times, folks! Basically, this guy was a Sufi philosopher, and Sufi really just means he's into all that spiritual stuff. And you know me, folks, I'm all about the spiritual stuff— especially the American spirit!

Ibn al-Arabi was big on this idea of "oneness," or as he would have said back then, "uno." That's some Spanish for you, bet you didn't know that. He believed that everything in the world is actually just one thing, and that we're all part of that one thing. It's like how we're one big country at the end of the day, and although some of us might be not so very smart and hate America, they still choose to live here because it's the greatest place on Earth. But here's where it gets really interesting. Ibn al-Arabi believed that God, or excuse me, "Dio," is part of the oneness, too. He thought that God is not some separate being up in the sky, but instead, God is actually everything. And you know what, folks? I gotta say, I kinda like that idea. I mean, I'm pretty great, right? So, if I'm everything, and God is

Trumping Philosophy | 76

everything, that means I'm basically God. Just saying. There's a reason so many of these angry satanic leftists don't like me.

But seriously, this guy had some pretty radical ideas. He said that all religions are really just different ways of talking about the same thing, and that there's no one "right" religion. Now, I know some of my supporters might not like hearing that, but let me tell you, folks, it takes a big man to admit that there's more than one way of doing things. And I'm a big man, believe me. Now, those ways might be wrong, but it's part of the freedom of this country to let people be wrong. Just remember, folks, they're gonna be judged elsewhere. And speaking of judgement, Ibn al-Arabi also thought there were these "perfect humans" that could help the other smaller people figure out the right thing to do. And honestly, folks, I see that every day. I always knew there was a reason that I had billions of dollars, and if spending a lot of it to become the president isn't the best way to help others understand the right way to do things, I don't know what is.

Anyway, that's Ibn al-Arabi in a nutshell. And another thing he said is "you can tell a lot about a man by the company he keeps." Well, Ibn al-Arabi kept some pretty good company. He was buddies with some of the greatest philosophers and thinkers of his time, the real MAGAs of long ago. And you know who else keeps good company? That's right, folks: yours truly. I keep you real American patriots in my company, and that's how we're going to make this country great.

Shinran

Alright, let's talk about Shinran, folks, which I think is a pretty fun name. Sounds like something out of a cartoon. He was a Japanese Buddhist monk who founded the Jodo Shinshu, or in real words, that means "True Pure Land school." It's kind of a clunky name for a school— maybe he could've tried something like Shinran University— but this guy was a real genius, believe me. He came up with this idea that enlightenment was actually a gift from Amida Buddha. That's right, folks, a gift! You don't have to do anything, just sit back and wait for enlightenment to be delivered right to your doorstep. It's like Amazon Prime, but for spiritual awakening.

Now, some people might say that sounds a little too good to be true, but trust me, folks, Shinran was the real deal. He had a huge following, people loved him. He was like the Elvis of Buddhism, only without the hip gyrations. Or maybe with them. Who knows! They didn't have news back then. But here's the thing, folks, just like Elvis, Shinran was also a rebel. He wasn't afraid to speak his mind and go against the establishment. He believed that Buddhism had become too rigid and dogmatic, and he wanted to shake things up a bit— again, just like Elvis and the hips!

And let me tell you, he did just that. He even went so far as to criticize other Buddhist teachers of his time. Can you believe that? This guy had more guts than a chicken farm, even though he was probably vegetarian. And you know what? People loved him for it. They loved that he was honest and authentic, even if it meant going against the grain. It's like when I speak my mind, folks. People might not always agree with me, but they know I'm not just saying what the establishment wants me to say. It's the losers out there who want to keep me— and us— quiet that really need to brush up with a class at Shinran University. Maybe Don Lemon and Jake Tapper could use some True Pure Land school!

Saint Thomas Aquinas

So, we've got this guy Thomas Aquinas. Some people call him "Saint" Thomas Aquinas, but honestly, I don't see what's so saintly about him. He's just a guy who wrote a lot of books and stuff, you know? He's got some ideas about God and religion, but honestly, I think my ideas are way better. Trust me, folks. I could write an even better version of the Bible if I wanted to. It would be set in America instead of the Middle East or whatever! The Israel bits are okay, though. I might keep them. But I wouldn't go too far— the last time some guy tried that; it ended up creating RINO Mitt Romney!

Anyway, so Aquinas was this big-shot philosopher and theologian back in the day. He was all about combining Christian beliefs with Greek philosophy, which like I've said before, folks, you just can't do. Doesn't work. You think Jesus would get along with Zeus? Gimme a break. Honestly, I think Aquinas coulda used a few more ideas from yours truly. He was really into this thing called natural law, where some rules are just built into the universe. Like, you don't have to be told not to murder someone - it's just wrong, you know? Although honestly, I could probably get away with it. I guess it's a good idea and all to just follow what makes sense, but honestly, I think it's pretty obvious that I'm the one who's really good at making laws, even perhaps better than nature might be. I mean, look at all the executive orders I've signed. Those are some great laws, let me tell you.

Oh, and another thing about Aquinas - he was really into this idea that faith and reason could work together. Like, you could use your brain to figure out things about God, but you also had to have faith in Him. And I guess that's okay, but honestly, I think it's pretty obvious that I've got the best brain. The biggest brain, really. And I don't need faith in anything to know that I'm right. What happens when I put my faith in God, and then he ends up being wrong about something? How am I supposed to explain that to the American people?

So yeah, that's Not-So-Saint Thomas Aquinas for you— a lousy guy generally. He's got some ideas, I guess, but honestly, they're not as great as mine. If he had just listened to me, he could have been a lot more successful. He might've been Saint Aquinas, but he was never President Aquinas, so what does that tell you, huh?

Jon Duns Scotus

Alright, let's talk about this Jon Duns Scotus guy. First off, I gotta say, what a terrible name. I mean, who in their right mind names their kid Jon Duns Scotus? It's like they were trying to make him sound smart before he even did anything. Now, I know a lot about Scotus, believe me. I appointed three of its members. But here's the deal about Jon. Just like our John on our Scotus, he's a little bit wishy-washy.

He was apparently some big shot philosopher in the Middle Ages. I don't know if you've heard of him, but I'm sure he's huge in the academic world— just not the real world! He had this thing called the "univocity of being," and I don't know about you, but that seems like a pretty hard word to understand. For others, I mean. I have the best words, of course, I know all of them.

Basically, he means we can talk about and describe everything the same way. And you know what? That's a pretty dumb idea if you ask me. I mean, you wouldn't talk about me the way you'd talk about Sleepy Joe, right? Even the other members of the radical left, they've all got their own names. Some are sleepy, some are crooked, some are low energy. It makes a difference, folks!

But here's the thing, he was also a big believer in this thing called "haecceity". Yeah, you heard me right, "haecceity." That's just a fancy way of saying individuality, and at that point, why not just say that? That's what happens when you get way too obsessed with legal talk like Scotus. Now, I gotta admit, that's a little more interesting to me. I mean, I'm all about being an individual and doing things my own way. After all, doing things collectively is just some radical socialist way of thinking, and we don't want that, no we don't. He also thought there was this other thing called the "principle of individuation," which really just sounds like the same damn thing as before, but this time, it's about how things have properties that make them different from other things. Of course, they do, Jon, they're different things! You don't need to be a philosopher to figure that out!

Overall, I don't know what to make of this Jon Duns Scotus character. On the one hand, he had some interesting ideas about individuality. But on the other hand, he was all about this univocity of being nonsense, which just sounds like a bunch of academics trying to sound smart. Now, what Scotus does isn't quite in line with that whole individual thing, especially since today it's made up of five very fine people— three especially great ones— one flaky guy, and three radical leftist ladies. Sad!

William of Ockham

So, William of Ockham was a big deal in the 14th century, and he came up with this thing called "Ockham's Razor." Now, some people think that's a shaving tool, but it's actually a way to figure stuff out. So, here's the deal; when you're trying to solve a problem, you gotta use the simplest explanation possible. That means you don't wanna go adding a bunch of extra stuff. It's like when I'm building a big, beautiful wall. I don't waste time and money on things like "offices" or "pathways to citizenship." I just want a big, beautiful wall that does its job. That's what William of Ockham was all about—keeping it simple. Ockham would probably like the wall a lot. He'd say "Don, this is incredible. It's just like my razor. You used the simplest idea, just incredible."

Now, some not-so-smart people who have some maybe not-very-good ideas might say, "Shouldn't we try some of these ideas?" But try telling that to William of Ockham and see how far you get. He'd say that if you can explain something simply, you should just go with it. Because the thing is, if someone comes up with some crazy idea that's hard to understand, it's always gonna end up creating a problem. It's like when the Radical Un-American Left wants to pass all these complicated bills that just ruin our country, and when nobody understands them, it's a total disaster. Sad!!

Now, those same low IQ people might be thinking, "Why do we care?" Well, William of Ockham really set the stage. If he didn't show how important it was for us to think simply, we never would've had this great beautiful country, and more importantly, your favorite president! When the British were doing stuff we didn't like, did we try to come up with some complicated explanation for how to solve it? No! We just kicked their asses. So, folks, if you ever find yourself in a difficult situation—and believe me, I've been in a lot of them (WITCH HUNT!!)— just remember William of Ockham and his trusty razor. And if all else fails, just build a big, beautiful wall. He'd love it, believe me.

Machiavelli

Okay, folks, we're gonna talk about Machiavelli, one of the most famous Italian guys ever. Now, some people say he was a total jerk, but let me tell you, this guy was a genius when it came to politics. He wrote this book called *The Prince* that's basically a guide to ruling properly. He basically says that if you wanna be a successful leader, you gotta be tough. You gotta be willing to do whatever it takes to stay in power, even if it means doing some things that might not be so nice. Believe me, I've seen when things aren't nice. Sometimes you gotta hurt people pretty badly. It's like when I had bone spurs during Vietnam. Put me out of commission for a long time, a long time. It's like when I'm negotiating a big business deal. I'm not gonna let some other guy push me around. I'm gonna be tough and get what I want. That's what Machiavelli was all about - being a strong, fearless leader.

Now, some people might say, "Hey, Don, isn't it important to be kind and compassionate as a leader?" But Machiavelli would say, "Wrong!" (in my best impression of him). He'd say that being too nice can actually be a weakness. Just look at Crazy Bernie— he's always talking about helping people, but it just makes him frail and cranky! Sad!

Now some people in the lame-stream news media have called me and my presidency Machiavellian, which I think is a really nice thing, really. I wasn't afraid to fire people who weren't doing their job. And I certainly wasn't afraid to take on the Radical Democrats. And everything at the border? That's the kind of leadership that Machiavelli would have admired.

So, folks, if you wanna be a successful leader, take a page out of Machiavelli's book (literally). Be tough, be strong, and don't be afraid to make the hard choices. I know a thing or two about leadership, believe me, and this guy really knows his stuff.

Wang Yangming

So, this guy Wang Yangming was a Chinese philosopher back in the day, and I gotta say, that's a pretty Chinese name. I mean, when you know China as well as I do, you meet a lot of Wangs and Yangs and Mings, but all together it's a lot. It's like if there was a guy with three English names, like John Paul Steven or something. Now, some people who don't know a lot about me— or about anything really— might ask whether I know anything about this guy. But let me tell you, I know a lot. I've done business with China, I've had some great Chinese food, and I've even built a great wall.

So, here's the deal, according to Wang Yangming. If you wanna be a good person, you gotta listen to your heart and go with your gut. It's like when I'm negotiating a deal. I don't just use my brain, I use my gut too. And let me tell you, my gut is never wrong. I have the best gut, the best. I can stomach nearly anything, especially everything the media very unfairly says.

Now you might be asking whether it's important to use your head, too, but Wang would say that your heart is the most important thing. You gotta trust your emotions and let them guide you. It's like when I'm tweeting. I don't think too much about it, I just let my fingers do the talking. And it always works out great. Some of the best written words out there. Really phenomenal stuff. I'd win a Pulitzer if they weren't all leftist hacks. Sad!

Francis Bacon

Okay, folks, we're gonna talk about Francis Bacon, one of the most important thinkers in history. Just terrific, really. Now, some people— and let's be honest here, some not-very-smart people— might say, "Hey, Don, what do you know about Bacon?" But let me tell you, I know a lot. I love bacon. Bacon is fantastic. Bacon is probably the best food ever invented. Come to Trump Tower, and you'll believe me. Bacon-wrapped Trump steaks.

But we're not talking about the food today, folks, as beautiful as it might be. We're talking about Francis Bacon, the guy who— well, basically invented— should I say invented? He basically invented the scientific method. Now, some people might say, "Hey, Don, what do you know about science?" But let me tell you, I know a lot. I've got a really good brain, one of the best there is. You know, they've studied it. They've looked at my DNA and they said it's not DNA, it's USA. Believe me, I'm always thinking about things. That's how you get rich. We might not know everything— we know a lot more than you all know and that's because the Democrats don't want to tell you, the American people, about it—but I've got a lot of theories.

Trumping Philosophy| 90

So, here's the deal, folks, here's the deal. According to Francis Bacon. If you wanna know something, you gotta use your brain. Now, not a lot of people can use their brain the way that Bacon did, or the way I do, but you're smart people. You're my people, so I know you're smart people. You gotta come up with a hypothesis, or as I like to call it— a big idea, test it, and then draw a conclusion. It's like when I'm trying to figure out if a business deal is gonna be a winner or a loser. I do my research, I gather my data, and then I make a decision. I have the best people in the world help me do that, and sometimes they give me a lot of good stuff, and that's what we call peer review, folks— peer review. Sometimes they aren't always the best, though, and that's when you gotta come up with a new idea and a new hypothesis. That's what Francis Bacon was all about - using your brain to figure things out.

Now, some people might say, "Hey, Don, isn't it important to have faith too?" And I know you're all good people, good Christian people, but Francis Bacon would say, "No way, José!" (or whatever they said in England back then). He'd say that faith is nice and all, but it's not gonna get you anywhere in life. Now I know a lot of great folks with faith who've done really well; you know that fella Osteen? Really nice guy, really nice. Almost as nice as me. Rich as me though? Not so much. Now Bacon, he had a nice amount of money too, but he wasn't so much worried about doing as he was about thinking. He said—and I think these are his exact words— you gotta use your brain, you gotta gather your evidence, and you gotta come up with a conclusion. That's how you make progress.

That's kinda like when I was president; remember those beautiful days? I was always thinking, always strategizing, always coming up with new ideas. I wasn't afraid to take risks or challenge the status quo. And let me tell you, it worked out pretty well for me. We made the best deals, the best decisions. You look at what we did in cases like Russia, like China. We hypothesize that they're ripping us off in trade, we gather our evidence by looking at what's happened to our once great and beautiful cities, and we conclude that something needs to be done about it— and we did!

Now, some people might be thinking, "Okay, Don, we get it. Francis Bacon was all about using your brain. But why do we care about some old English dude?" After all, our beautiful country is here because we didn't listen to some very nasty English people, and if we did, then you wouldn't have your favorite president. Well, here's the thing you gotta understand, folks. Francis Bacon was ahead of his time. He knew that if you wanna make progress, you gotta use your brain. You gotta think critically and come up with new ideas. And that's the kind of leadership that we need more of these days - bold, innovative, and unafraid to think outside the box— not sleepy or low energy.

So, if you wanna be successful, use your brain. Come up with a hypothesis, test it, and then draw a conclusion. And if all else fails, just remember that I'm always here to give you some advice. I know a thing or two about having a big brain, I can tell you that much.

Thomas Hobbes

Thomas Hobbes, Thomas Hobbes. A great comic strip named after this guy. Half of it, anyway. Now, some people might not know who this guy is, but let me tell you, he's a big deal. He wrote a book called *Leviathan*, and it's all about politics and stuff. Now, I gotta say, his understanding of politics is pretty smart. He said that people are basically selfish and greedy. And you know what, folks? I kinda agree with him. I mean, look at me. I'm a billionaire. Do you think I got here by being nice? No! I got here by being the best, and the most ruthless. And that's what Hobbes was talking about – if you want to get ahead, you gotta trample others, even if you'd otherwise get along. In politics, it's the same. Low energy Jeb, Lyin' Ted, Little Marco? I have a great relationship with them now, but when they were against me? Ruthless, gotta be ruthless.

Now, many people are saying that this might go against what we call "democracy." Have you heard of this, folks, democracy? Big word. Big word for a big country. A lot of people seem to like it. But let me tell you, folks, democracy is overrated, especially when it's so easily rigged by the Democrats. We gotta remember that we are a Republic! And they talk about the voting. Well voting— if you don't do it securely and the right way— is just an opportunity to let people who hate America steal power away from real American patriots like you. That's why we need a strong leader like me. I know how to get things done. And if anyone gets in my way, you know what I tell them? "You're fired." It's that easy. But back to Hobbes. He really had the right idea when it came to pushing others around. We need more philosophers like that. Too many of these others are just all about holding hands and being one with the universe. Hobbes knew that the only way to control people is to have a strong leader. And that's exactly what I am, folks. A strong leader. The best leader ever, some might say.

Rene Descartes

Alright, folks, we're talking about Rene Descartes here. Some people might say, "Who's Rene Descartes?" But let me tell you, he's a big deal. He was a philosopher, mathematician, and all-around smart guy. You also gotta make sure you're pronouncing it right— the French are really particular about it. I met their president—great guy, nice guy— and apparently his name isn't "macaron." So this guy, Descartes, isn't actually pronounced how it's written, which I think, frankly, is kind of ridiculous. So, you actually say it: day-cart. I know, I know. It's a much less cool name, and honestly, sounds like the name of a loser. I'm not sure why the French are so scared of the letter "s" but seems like they can't get over it.

So, here's the deal with Descartes. He said that the only way to know for sure that something is true is to doubt everything else, which doesn't make a whole lotta sense to me. But Descartes' crazy ideas didn't stop there, folks. He said that the only thing you can be absolutely certain of is that you exist. You know, like his famous phrase "I think, therefore I am." So what? Big freakin' deal. What am I supposed to say? "Wow, that's great, I know that I'm real now! Thank you, Rene!" By the way, that's a girl's name.

And you know what, folks? I'm pretty certain that I exist, and that I'm the best thing that ever happened to this country. Maybe France would do a lot better if they had someone like me, but no, they've got guys with women's names pointing out the obvious. Sad!

John Locke

Alright, folks, today we're talking about John Locke. Some people might say, "Who's John Locke?" But let me tell you, he's a big deal. He was a philosopher, political theorist, and all-around smart guy.

So, here's the deal. Locke said that people have natural rights, like the right to life, liberty, and property. And you know what, folks? I kinda agree with him. I mean, who doesn't want to be free and have lots of money? That's what our Constitution is all about, after all. The winners can be winners and the losers can be losers. It's all about responsibility folks, but the Democrats just want to take all that away! But Locke didn't stop there. He said that the purpose of government is to protect those natural rights. And that's exactly what I did. I protected people's rights. You see all these riots and these protestors, and I brought in law and order. That's the only way to protect people's rights — aggressive policing tactics. I made America great again. Believe me.

Let me tell you, folks, some people who disagree with Locke might parade around the idea of a "social contract," which is really just some overrated kumbaya bull used to bring in a whole load of radical socialism. It's just a bunch of people agreeing to be ruled by the government, and you know what type of people enjoy that? Losers!

So, the deal is, Locke knew that people have natural rights, and that the government's job is to protect them. And you know what, folks? That's exactly what I did. Despite what the fake news media and Soros-funded interests might tell you, I protected people's rights. I made America great again. Especially for you lovely people.

Benedict de Spinoza

Alright, folks, Benedict de Spinoza. Now, you might be thinking to yourself that this is another one of those Spanish guys, but actually, he's from Portugal. Now, I don't know if there's much of a difference; after all, they speak the same language. But Benny here was big on this thing he called rationalism. He said that God and nature are the same thing, which I think is really smart. I mean, I love nature. I have the best golf courses, the best hotels, and the best resorts. And you know what makes them so great? Nature, folks. He said that everything in the universe follows the laws of nature. And you know what, folks? We're in the universe. And he seems to be on the right track! I mean, I'm a winner, and winners always follow the laws of nature. After all, you don't see any losers owning golf courses and resorts, do you?

Now, a lot of people tend to be worried about religion when we talk too much about rationalism. But let me tell you, folks, religion is overrated, and Spinoza knew that. He said that we don't need religion to understand the universe. We just need reason and logic, two of my favorite words, two of the best words, really. I'm a very logical person. I make the best decisions. Just ask anyone. So at the end of the day, Portugal seems to be pretty good when it comes to their philosophers.

They really seem to have the right idea. Maybe— and I don't say this lightly— one of my favorite types of Mexicans. Benedict de Spinoza, he's really up there for me.

Leibniz

Listen folks, let me tell you about Leibnetz, okay? It's a tremendous concept, truly tremendous. Now, I don't know if you've heard about it, but I've been briefed on it by some really tremendously smart people, and it's a real game changer, believe me. This guy named Gottfried Wilhelm Leibniz came up with it. Great guy, by the way, really smart. Those Germans, real hardworking people. Real hardworking. Always follow through. Some people who don't pay close attention to things the way I do might call it Leibniz, but trust me, Leibnetz is how you say it, okay? It's like people saying the difference between "Trump" and "America." Two very similar things, but they are in fact different words. Now, Leibnetz, it's all about seeing the world as interconnected, like a big web. See, Leibniz believed that there's this harmony in the universe, like everything, and I mean everything, is linked together in some way. It's like a big cosmic network, folks.

And he even came up with this idea called the "monad," which is like these little pieces that are all part of this grand design. I'm a monad, you're a monad, even Sleepy Joe is a monad! Now, Leibniz was way ahead of his time. He came up with this idea back in the 17th century, can you believe it? But let me tell you, his philosophy is still relevant today. It's all about understanding the connections between things, seeing the bigger picture. And you know what, I've always been a big believer in connections. I know how to make connections, believe me. In business, in politics, you name it. Sometimes my business IS connected to politics, and that's when the Radical Left comes after me! That's what Leibnetz is all about, folks.

Giambattista Vico

So, Giambattista Vico, a real great Italian name. I once knew a Vico— best Italian deli in Manhattan. Real great guy. Not doing so great now, though, thanks to Creepy Cuomo! Some people might not know who this guy is, but let me tell you, folks, he's a big deal. He said that history is cyclical, which I think is really insightful. I mean, look at all the things I did during my presidency. I made America great again. But you know what's even better? Making America great again, again. And that's exactly what I'm gonna do. We're gonna have a big, beautiful, cyclical history. It's gonna be tremendous, folks. Because you know what happens when we make America great again, again? We get to win again! We're gonna have so many cycles, it's gonna be so tremendous, and we're gonna make the country so great that you're gonna say "Mr. President, please, can we stop with the cycles?" But I'll say "No, we can't! We have to keep making American great again, again, again!"

Vico was really good at arguing against the "Divine Providence" too, folks, just incredible at it. He said that human beings have the power to shape their own destiny. And you know what, folks? That's exactly what I did during my presidency. I shaped America's destiny. I made it great again. And I'm gonna keep doing that, folks. Believe me. But Vico didn't stop there. He said that human beings create their own history through their actions. And you know what, folks? I agree with that too. I mean, I'm a man of action. I don't just sit around and talk. I get things done. And that's why America loves me. They know that I'm always working for them.

And what kind of an idea is "Divine Providence" anyway? I didn't see much of it when the Democrats stole the election from me! If God was really pulling all the strings, we wouldn't have seen such an injustice. I know that, you know that, the Satanic Left know that, and Vico knows that!

George Berkeley

Alright, folks, today we're talking about George Berkeley. Now, I don't know about you, but I've done some digging into this Berkeley name, and apparently, that school has produced a TON of Democrat judges and politicians who want to destroy our country. One hell of a legacy you've got there, George, what a shame, what a shame. Some of the most disastrous politicians came out of this place, ruining our once beautiful state of California with its crime and its drugs. Some real thinkers there, it seems. Just wait until they actually reach the United States.

So, here's the deal with Berkeley. He said that the world only exists because we perceive it, and that's really on the money. I mean, I've built a huge empire based on perception. That's what branding is all about, folks. Making people think you're the best, even if you're not. But you know what? I am the best. I'm the best president ever. It's so true that everybody perceives it. Everybody. Berkeley also went on to say that things only exist when we perceive them, and again, he's got a pretty clear idea of how things work. You know why the Trump brand is the best? Because people perceive it that way. I'm a master of perception. I know how to make people see things the way I want them to see them. That's how I won the election, folks. Perception is everything.

So although the school might be one of— if not the— worst things to happen to our country, George Berkeley seemed to have the right idea. It's not about what's true, but what people perceive is true.

Charles Louis de Secondat

Alright, let's talk about Charles Louis de Secondat. I'd give him a nickname, but he already came up with one for himself— Montesquieu. You wanna know why that name sounds so ridiculous? He was French. And you know how I feel about the French, folks. They're just jealous of America because we've got everything, they've got but better. French bread, French fries— even the Eiffel Tower in Las Vegas. But despite that whole French thing, I kinda like Montesquieu. He said that power should be divided among different branches of government, so that no one has too much power. He called it checks and balances, two beautiful words, checks and balances. That's why I'm always talking about the Deep State and the Fake News Media, which are really like the fourth and fifth branches, and that's why I need to keep them in check. Imagine if Congress and the Lame-stream News and the FBI were able to stop me from doing all the amazing things I did for this country. We'd have no wall, no economy, and a country full of crime and drugs. Sad!

Montesquieu was also real big on the branches being separate and independent— and I'm all about independence. America First, folks, remember that. We don't need anyone else telling us how to run our country, and we don't need the other branches trying to get in the way of the executive. Montesquieu was also a big believer in liberty, which is an idea that I like very much. He said something real smart in French one time, and I have people close to me saying that when you translate it, it comes out as "people should be able do what they want, as long as they're not hurting anyone." To me, that sounds like Montesquieu would've been a Republican. We need to let people be who they want to be, and do what they want to do— that's the only way to fight the radical woke ideology.

David Hume

So next up is David Hume. Now, let me tell you folks, this guy was a philosopher from Scotland. And you know what? Scotland is a beautiful place, folks. Let me tell you, the golf courses are fantastic, especially the Trump ones. My mother was from Scotland, too, so in a way, I feel really at home with the ideas there. Some could say, maybe, that I was Scotland's greatest contribution to the world, especially when you look at all the wonderful things that happened there. I don't think they could've gotten Brexit done without me, and just look at Boris Johnson. It's like they cloned me!

But back to Hume. The guy was all about skepticism, questioning everything and such. And you know what, folks? That's not a bad thing. I'm always questioning things too. Like, why do I have to listen to Congress, or why can't I stay in office when the Democrats so obviously rigged it? But you know what, folks? That's not how it works, no matter how much easier it would be otherwise. Now, Hume was also all about causation. He said that we can't really know if one thing causes another. That's just crazy talk. Of course, one thing causes another! Like when I tweet, the stock market goes up. That's causation, folks. I am the best causationer. No one causes things the way I do.

Hume was all about empiricism, too. That means you only believe what you can see and touch. Like when I said there was voter fraud in the 2020 election. I had evidence, folks. I just didn't show it to anyone. That's how they did it with the voting machines. If you look at the numbers, not the fake numbers that the Democrats put there, but the real numbers before all the mail-in people voted, you can see that I won. If it wasn't for those extra people who voted against me, everyone would've seen that I won fair and square. It's such a shame, folks, such a shame. You know, if Hume was there, he would've said that we can't see and touch the votes from the machines, which is really the problem. But no, now we've got the Sleepiest and Worst president maybe ever. And it all could've been avoided if we listened to Hume.

Rousseau

Jean-Jacques Rousseau, let me tell you, this guy was a total loser. He was a philosopher from Switzerland, and you know what they say about Switzerland? Boring! Absolutely boring, folks. It's a wishy-washy country, never taking sides when it really counts. But let me tell you, their banks? Phenomenal. Most secure and safe place ever. You can't even tell what's in them, which is really handy when it comes to doing your taxes.

But let's talk about Rousseau's ideas. He was all about this thing called the "social contract," which we already said was total bogus. Why should we give away our freedom to people who just want to force their radical woke ideas on us! Just look at the word itself! See it there? Social! It's socialism, folks, don't let them fool you! Same thing with his ideas about the "general will." No way should the government look out for everyone. You gotta pull yourself up by your bootstraps, folks, or else you're just gonna end up like a loser like Rousseau.

Rousseau also said that people are born good, but society corrupts them. And you know what, folks? That's just not true. Look at me. I was born great, and I've only gotten better.

Society didn't corrupt me. In fact, I'm making society better, folks. That's just what I do.

But you know what, folks? Rousseau also said that people should live simple lives, and not be so focused on material things. And you know what? That's just ridiculous. Material things are great, folks. I have the best things. The thingiest things. That's the real key to being happy, take it from me. I've got the best happiness, the best temperament.

Rosseau might think I'd like him because of his whole Swiss thing, but just like the cheese, his ideas are full of holes and totally stink. They wouldn't work for America, and the more the Radical Left keeps pushing them, the worse it's gonna be.

Kant

Alright, folks, we're talking about Immanuel Kant, and let me tell you, he was a real loser. He was a philosopher from Germany, and you know what they say about Germany? Overrated, folks. Absolutely overrated. Full of Globalists nowadays who just want the US to pay for everything!

Kant was all about the "categorical imperative," which is basically that we should always act how we would want everyone else to act. In other words, it's the Golden Rule, folks, the Golden Rule. And I know a lot about gold. Just take a look at my penthouse, my buildings, or anything I do. Gold is the way to go, folks. Especially when it comes to currency. Now I know gold better than anybody, and this sure isn't the way to go about getting it. If you really want to be a winner, you're gonna have to make some tough decisions, and a lot of losers aren't going to like you, complaining about "unfairness" and "unsafe working conditions" and "OSHA violations." Loser talk! Kant also talked a lot about "duty," which is really just code for owing somebody something. That's not a great position to be in, folks, just look at our national debt and our trade deficits. Something tells me Kan't-Do Kant wouldn't be able to fix that! He said that we have a duty to always do what's right, no matter what. And you know what, folks?

Trumping Philosophy | 113

That's just not practical. Sometimes you have to make tough decisions, and doing what's right isn't always the easiest thing. But here's the way around it, folks. The right thing might be the right thing for yourself. So, if you're always doing what will make you come out on top, you're fulfilling your duty.

So, you know, Kant had some interesting ideas, but they just don't work in the real world. You can't be a successful leader by following some made-up rules. You gotta live in the real world. You have to be a winner, and sometimes, yes, that means being a little mean, or saying some pretty aggressive things, or taking away legally required benefits. That's what I do every day, folks. I'm a winner, and that's just how it is.

Moses Mendelssohn

Okay, folks, next up is Moses Mendelssohn, a real nobody. I mean, who even is this guy? He's some philosopher from Germany who thought he really knew it all, but the truth is that his ideas are just a mess, folks, just a mess. Mendelssohn was all about this thing called "Jewish Enlightenment," have you heard about this? He thought that Jews should integrate into European society and be treated as equals. And you know what, folks? That's just not practical. Jews have been doing just fine on their own for centuries. They don't need some philosopher— especially a German one, talk about some awkward history— telling them what to do and how to live their lives. I live in New York, and believe me, the number of Jews here that are doing well is really tremendous— many of them donors to my campaign! Now why the hell would they want to move to Europe, especially considering how they've been treated there? The truth is, America has become the proper home of these people, more than any other nation on Earth.

Mendelssohn also talked about "rational religion," which is all about using your brain to work your way through your religious beliefs. And that's the right way to go about it, let me tell you. Really makes you think, at least he had some sense of a brain. You know, I'd almost like this guy for that, but you know what else? Mendelssohn was a real liberal, and I mean a big one. He believed in freely expressing your thoughts, which is just not how the world works. You have to be careful about what you say, especially when you're the People's President and all the media wants to do is lie and go on a Witch Hunt! The radical Democrats will come after you with their cancel culture and their censorship and their wokeness. The truth is that free speech is under attack, folks, and you gotta be careful who you're talking to. Massive Failure Mendelssohn just doesn't cut it. Not practical, not smart, and way too liberal! Sad!

Marquis de Condorcet

Alright, folks, we're talking about this guy Marquis de Condorcet. And let me tell you, he's a real loser. Even his parents thought so! I mean, who even names their kid Marquis? It's like he's trying too hard to be fancy. Guess that's just the way the French do it, especially considering they have to stand in the shadow of our great nation.

But let's talk about his ideas, folks. Condorcet was all about this thing called progress. And you know what, folks? If you look real close at that word, you can see it sounds a hell of a lot like "progressive," and that tells you all you need to know about that. Mark here is just not realistic. I mean, we already have everything we need in America, why do we need progress? We're already the greatest country in the world. What more do we need?

More books? Nah! Trust me, I've read all of 'em, and there's plenty information out there. He even wrote this book called "Sketch for a Historical Picture of the Progress of the Human Mind." I mean, who even has time to write a book that long? And who cares about the progress of the human mind anyway? We need to focus on the progress of America, folks. What good is a mind if it doesn't have a job to do? Are we just gonna let Mexico and China take those jobs away? No!

More science? Well now they're telling us that we have to "listen to the science," which basically just means "listen to the democrats." I'm sure as hell not listening to the democrats, so why would I want more science? It's all part of their agenda, folks. And get this, folks. Condorcet also believed in democracy; can you believe it? At the end of the day, he's just as much of a Democrat as the other scientists out there like Fauci. We already have everything we need in America, and we don't need some Un-American Democrat philosopher telling us how to live our lives.

Jeremy Bentham

Okay folks, let's talk about this guy Jeremy Bentham. He's a philosopher from the UK, and let me tell you, he's a real weirdo, which to be fair, can't be helped. He's English, after all.

Bentham was all about this thing called utilitarianism. And what is that, you ask? Well, apparently, it's this idea that we should do whatever is the best for the most amount of people. Sounds like some people-pleasing communism to me, folks. If Bentham had his way, all the socialists would take my money, and then no one would be happy! And get this, folks, to make it even more ironic. Bentham was all about the greatest happiness principle. He believed that we should always do what brings the most happiness, no matter what. So, which is it, Benny? Should we do what's best for all of your radical socialist friends, or what's best for me and other real Americans? I think I know which one I'm gonna go with.

And here's the craziest part, folks. Bentham thought that pleasure was the highest good. Can you believe it? He thought that pleasure was more important than anything else. And that's great sometimes, believe me, all of my wives have been some of the best women in America, and America's not the only place they've been the best in. I know pleasure more than anyone else. But you know what else, folks? Bentham was a real weirdo when it came to government, but I think in perhaps a good way. He believed in this thing called the Panopticon, which was basically a prison where the guards could watch the prisoners all the time. It's like a big zoo for all the prisoners, which I think might not be too bad of an idea. We gotta have law and order, folks, gotta have it.

Bentham might not be too sure what he wants, but at least he's got a good idea of how to keep things safe. England's gonna need it with all the crime, all the stabbings. Many such cases! And maybe we can learn a thing or two over here.

Hegel

Alright folks, let me tell you about this guy Hegel. He's a German philosopher, and let me tell you, he's not the most exciting guy out there. But I'll do my best to make it entertaining for you. Hegel was all about this thing called dialectics. And what is that, you ask? Well, apparently that means everything is changing and contradictory. Just like the Democrats. Always talking about changing America for the better, but ultimately making things worse. But you know what, folks? That's just too complicated. I like things simple, and I'm sure you do too.

And get this, folks. Hegel thought there was this World Spirit that guided the course of history. But you know what, folks? I think that's just a load of hogwash. The only spirit we need is the American Spirit, and the World Spirit sounds like some nasty Globalist plot to hurt our country and help our enemies. But I'm not gonna let Hagel and Soros get away with that, believe me.

But you know what else, folks? Hegel thought the state is the highest form of human society. Can you believe it? The highest form? Have you ever seen the government— other than when I was in charge— do one thing right? He thought that the government was gonna be the one to save us all. Just disgraceful. You know what I think of that, folks? I think Hagel just wants to take away our God-given freedoms, just like the Globalist elites want him to.

And let me tell you, folks, it was just horrible learning all this to tell you. Hegel was not a very exciting writer, I mean his books were so long and boring, and I don't think anyone actually enjoys reading them. At least the aides who briefed me on this didn't enjoy it.

So, the next time someone says something about Hegel (which frankly, might not be anytime soon, because who listens to this guy?), just know that they're a globalist coming for your freedoms. No other possibility, folks.

Schopenhauer

Alright folks, let me tell you about Schopenhauer. He's a German philosopher, and let me tell you, he's not the most exciting guy out there. But I'll do my best to make it entertaining for you. So, Schopenhauer was all about this thing called the will, which is this force that makes the whole universe work. Now, I don't know why someone with as complicated a name as Schopenhauer would believe in some guy named Will, but he sure as hell isn't my prophet!

And this Will guy is apparently a real downer because Schopenhauer believed that the world was a miserable place, just never-ending suffering and pain. Which, to be fair, you can much better understand when you consider that he didn't live in America. We're the oldest and greatest country on Earth; we have the best military in the world, the greatest economy in the world (no thanks to Barack!) and, of course, the best people in the world, despite there being some not-so great ones that we call Democrats. We should all be grateful for it, especially when some very nasty people are trying to take it away. Schopenhauer was really big on pessimism, thinking everything was doomed to fail, and that there was no hope for the future. But you know what, folks? I'm an optimist. As long as I'm in charge, everything is gonna get better. We can make America great again, and maybe Germany will be a little better too when our country gets back on track.

We don't need to be miserable, folks. We can be happy and successful, and we can make the world— and most importantly, America— a better place. So, let's make America great again!

Comte

All right, folks, let me tell you about this guy Comte. He's a French philosopher, and let me tell you, he's a little bit out there, really. He was all into this positivism stuff, where the only real knowledge is science knowledge. But you know what, folks? That's just ridiculous. There's a lot we can learn from other places, especially when the scientists are just Democrats in disguise. Commie Comte doesn't know anything about the real world. Sad!

And get this, folks— Comte thought society went through these different stages, from theological to the metaphysical to scientific. But you know what, folks? I think we're already in the best stage. We have the best people, the best ideas, the best country. We don't need to go through any more stages, we're already at the top. And believe me, I know all about stages. When you do that many rallies a day, you get real used to 'em.

Plus, Comte was big on making a "religion of humanity, " can you believe that? Replacing traditional religion with this new religion just to make everyone hold hands? It's crazy talk. I mean, what good is religion if it's gonna unite people? And let me tell you, folks, Comte was not a very practical guy. He never had a plan, never had one at all.

Commie Comte is one of many philosophers that just never had a chance, just like anyone who runs against me. Low energy, bad ideas, and no way to actually implement them.

John Stewart Mill

Okay, John Stuart Mill. Another British one. Let me tell you, lots of ideas coming out of that country. We might have to look into that place becoming the 51st state. Wouldn't that be something?

So, this guy Mill was another utilitarian, always trying to make the most people happy. We've talked about this before, but look, just because some other guy says it doesn't make it a better idea. These philosophers love to say that their ideas are so great because they all agree with each other, but that doesn't work on this mind right here. The most stable genius mind of them all.

But you know what, folks? Mill also believed in education. And you know what? So do I. Education is very important, and I think we need to make it great again. Too much of this Critical Race Theory and America-hating in our schools today, folks. A damn shame, and we need to fix it for our children. But you know what else, folks? I think we need to focus on practical education, not just theoretical stuff. We need to teach people how to make deals, how to build businesses, how to win bigly. That's the kind of education we need. I've done a great deal to help make this happen— in fact, on my construction sites I've employed a great many children under the age of 12. Smartest kids in the world now, believe me.

So as much as John Stuart Mill was all about utilitarianism, his ideas about education seemed to have it right. But you know what, folks? I can make those ideas even better. If John saw what I was doing with this country, he'd be proud.

Kierkegaard

Okay folks, Soren Kierkegaard, named after the absolute best ride at Disney World. This guy, good Danish guy, was all about the individual, and so am I, folks. I believe in putting America first, and that means putting the individual first. Because what is America? It's just a bunch of Americans. And real Americans are incredibly individuals.

And let me tell you, folks, Kierkegaard was all about living an authentic life. He lived in the present moment and was true to himself, and encouraged others to do so as well. But you know what? Sometimes, you have to put on a show to win bigly. That's just the way it is. Everything you see in the media, on the stage? It's all politicians lying to stay in power. And you know what? They're winning. I hate to say it, folks, but they are. That's why we've gotta fight back, and fight hard. Soren would've thought so, too. He's got Viking blood!

So, Soren was all about the individual and living authentically. He would have made a great Republican today, and I think that he would've made a great member of the campaign. He knew when to be truthful, and when to maybe not do that just the right amount. A big winner!

Karl Marx

Well folks, we've come to the grandfather of failures, and maybe my least favorite person on this whole list. Karl Marx was a big loser who thought he was some kind of genius, and other losers who think they're geniuses have been parroting his ideas for generations now. Crazy Bernie, Nasty Nancy, Sleepy Joe— they all come back to Marx. Really just the worst guy.

Just look at what he wanted to do— taking away people's property and the government owning everything. Can you believe it? And he wanted to do it all in the name of "equality" - what a joke! And let me tell you, he was a total hypocrite. He was all about uniting the workers of the world and all this commie gobbledygook, but he was from a wealthy family! He mooched off of his parents and never worked an honest real job in his life. I, however, started with nothing. I worked hard to get a loan from my father, and I built a massive business empire by building off of his. It's the American Dream— anyone can do it, as long as you aren't like Marx!

Marx talked big, going on about "class struggle" and the rich "exploiting" the workers. But let me tell you, the workers don't need some kook to fight in their name. They need the chance to succeed on their own, and that's what I'm working to do. That's what making America great again is all about! He talked about the workers owning the means of production, but the truth is, sometimes people just want to be told what to do. There are leaders, and there are followers. The leaders, like me, naturally move to the top. The followers just eat it all up. They couldn't handle my hardworking lifestyle!

Marx was a complete disaster— the founder of all the problems we have today. He was wrong about everything, and his ideas have been proven wrong time and time again. I'm making America great again, and the Marxists in this country just want to tear it all down.

Herbert Spencer

Oh boy, Herbert Spencer, what a guy. Let me tell you folks, he's a real gem. Some people say he's the father of social Darwinism, which if you ask me, just doesn't make a lot of sense. If he made something, he should have his name on it. That's my philosophy with my buildings, and Spencer should have followed. Call it social Spencerism or something!

So social Spencerism was this idea that society evolves like animals do, and that only the strong survive. It's like survival of the fittest, but for society. And you know what they say, I'm a very fit guy, especially when you look at all the other short and low energy guys who try to criticize me. So, I'd be at the top of the social pyramid. It's just common sense, folks. But here's the thing, social Spencerism was also related to this other idea called eugenics. Now, eugenics can teach Spencer a lot, you see, because I don't know a thing about the guy who came up with it, but I know his name is Eugene. Name things after yourself, folks. It's how I've got Don. Jr. But whoever Eugene is apparently thought that we should only let certain people have kids because they have the best genes. That's why I have so many kids. I mean, I have great genes, really tremendous.

But some people didn't like Spencer's ideas. They said that it just makes rich people get richer and poor people get poorer. But here's the thing, folks, if you're gonna be poor, it's because you're a loser, and if you're gonna stay a loser, of course you're gonna get poorer! But if you take my advice and become a winner, you'll get richer! It's that simple, and Spencer knew it.

So, you know, Spencer might not have had the insight to put his name on things, but it seems like he had the right idea about winners and losers. He just didn't have what it took in the end!

William Dilthey

William Dilthey? I mean, come on folks, have you ever heard of this guy? What kind of name is Dilthey anyway? Sounds like something my doctor would prescribe for my allergies— that is if I had any health issues in the first place! Clean bill of health, here, folks, totally exonerated! But seriously, he was some kind of philosopher from Germany, and he had this theory about understanding human beings and their experiences. Big whoop. Not like we haven't had a bunch of those already.

So Dilthey wasn't too sure about just using the scientific method; he also had this "hermeneutics" idea to interpret people's thoughts and feelings. I don't know why he thought he was a mind reader, but I can tell that it didn't work well, because if it did, he'd know how much everyone thought he was a total loser. But Dilthey didn't stop there. He also had this idea that history isn't a bunch of facts and dates, but it's actually a collection of human experiences. And you know, I think that's true for some people. I often think that I know exactly how Napoleon and other great men of history felt at their peak. But other people, the losers and the whiners of their day, no clue what they were thinking. It's just not in my genes, folks.

Anyway, I guess Dilthey had some fans, but to me he just sounds like another one of those boring philosophers who talk a lot but don't really say anything. Plus, less feeling, more doing. That's what I think!

William James

William James? Now that's a name I can get behind. Sounds like a winner to me. I mean, if you're going to have a philosopher name, might as well make it sound presidential, right? And that's two presidents in his name, so double the wisdom. So, what did this James guy have to say? Well, James was all about experiences shaping who we are, and trusting instincts when it comes down to it. And you know what, I can get behind that. I mean, look at me, I trust my gut all the time, the best decisions I've ever made. James seemed to have a clear idea of how to get things done, and I think he would've made a great running mate. Better than Little Mike Pence!

James also had this idea about "pragmatism," which is basically all about finding practical solutions to problems instead of getting your head stuck in the clouds. And you know what, that's exactly the kind of approach we need in politics. No more conversations about what's "feasible" or "ethical" or "constitutional," let's just get stuff done. You know, James would be really great on the campaign trail. James had a spiritual side, too, so he'd really help me in the parts of the country where they're really into that kind of stuff. He thought there was more to life than just what we can see, and we should embrace this big wonderful world we live in and all of its mysteries. Now, I'm not really a "mystery" guy, but hey, James can do what he wants. I don't expect a running mate of mine to be the same as me; after all, it would be a problem for me if he was, right? Can't have two people at the top of the ticket.

Overall, I think James had some good ideas, good values. And you know what, I think those are values that we could all use more of in today's world. So here today I'm announcing to all of you lovely people that my running mate for this election will be philosopher William James. Let's give him a hand, why don't we?

Folks, I'm writing this section after I've been informed by my aides of a great tragedy. It appears that would-be future Vice President William James has died. It appears that he passed on during the early hours of August 26, 1910, which is really just a shame. If he had stuck things out a little longer, we would've done some great things together. Rest in peace to a real American Patriot!

Nietzsche

Alright, listen up folks, we're talking about Nietzsche. Big philosopher, very important. But let me tell you, he's not my favorite. Why? Well, he's got this whole idea of the "ubermensch," which is apparently German for Superman. He thought that there would be one man who could rise above all the others, and you know, folks, that reminds me of a certain someone today. I'm not gonna say who it is, as we all know how humble I am, but I'm just gonna throw that out there.

Now, Nietzsche is always going on about how God is dead. And you know what? He's right. After all, what is God if not a part of the American Dream, and if the American Dream is dead, then why would God have somehow made it out okay? So, Nietzsche might have been right about that one. But it doesn't have to be that way. Obama and Sleepy Joe and the Democrats may have killed God, but I, Donald J. Trump promise that I can bring him back. I very humbly offer myself up to be the new God. I've had some of the most important jobs in the world, and I gotta say, I don't think there's anyone else more qualified to fill the big man's shoes.

But you know, Nietzsche does have some good points too. He talks a lot about the will to power, and I gotta say, I have a lot of that. I mean, look at all the things I've accomplished. I beat Crooked Hillary, I beat the fake news media, and I even beat COVID faster and more definitively than anyone else ever has. My body is nearly indestructible, folks, and that's what happens when according to Nietzsche, you're both God and Superman.

And let's not forget about his idea of the "eternal recurrence." Now, I'm not sure I totally understand it, but I think it's like, what if everything happened over and over again, forever? And you know what, that's not such a bad idea. Because every time it happens, I'll be in charge. We can keep making America great, over and over. Every time one of those Radical Democrats gets into office and kills God, I'll come back next time to win. And I'll win big, folks.

You know, Nietzsche really had the right idea when it came to predicting how well I was going to do. He knew there was gonna be a Superman, he knew that God was gonna lose to Obama, and he knew that I was gonna come along and fix it all. Really smart guy. Has my complete and total endorsement!

Frege

Alright, folks, let me tell you about this guy Frege, okay? He's a philosopher, but nobody really knows what the hell he's talking about. I mean, seriously, have you seen his work? It's like he's trying to create a whole new language just to confuse people. We speak English here! He had these ideas about "sense" and "reference," but it seems like the guy had no sense at all, and I sure as hell wouldn't give him a reference. This is what happens when you go against what our country stands for, folks. Big loser energy.

But here's the thing, he's considered one of the fathers of modern logic. And you know what I think about logic? It's overrated bigly. You don't need logic when you've got instinct, and I've got great instincts, the best instincts. And get this, he thought that math was really just a branch of logic, which makes no sense at all. When I'm making deals, I'm not asking about what percent of what should go where, we're here to talk *business,* and business isn't math. You want to succeed, folks? Don't worry about the math, that's what you hire people for.

And, you know, some— frankly, gullible— people just go on about how Frege made all these math symbols and equations, but I don't think that makes you smart, I think that makes you wasteful. When you make new equations, you gotta have people to do those equations, and they could be doing something a lot better than that!

So, at the end of the day, Frege was a philosopher who liked to overcomplicate and confuse regular people with his fancy symbols and weird ideas about language and logic. It's really a total disaster, folks, nothing good came from it at all. Sad!

Edmund Husserl

Alright, let's talk about this Husserl guy. First of all, let me tell you, Husserl is a phenomenologist. It's basically when you study things that happen, and you all already know that I'm the best at making things happen. Business deal? I've done more than anyone else. Elections won? I'm two for two, folks. Capitols sieged? The biggest in history, no one ever did it better. Husserl's big on this idea of intuition, which, frankly, is something that I have in spades. I have the best intuition. It's huge.

Now, Husserl thought there's a difference between the way things looks and the way they actually are. It's kind of like a Democrat voting machine. And he takes a closer look though this thing he calls "eidetic reduction," and I'm telling you, I'm the best at reducing things. Your taxes? Reduced those. My taxes? Reduced them to zero all my life. And let me tell you, folks, that doesn't make me bad, that makes me smart. If you can see how to reduce something here and there, you should do it. Makes everything a whole lot easier.

But you know what, Husserl wasn't always clear about what he wanted. He talked about things like "bracketing" and

Trumping Philosophy | 143

"phenomenological reduction," which just sound way too confusing. Frankly, I think he just likes to use big words to sound smart. And like I said before, the dictionary, the best book I ever read. I know all the words. Merriam Webster himself is one of my top guys. But Husserl's words? Never heard of them. Fake news!

Overall, Husserl is a bit of a snooze-fest, if you ask me. He studies doing things, but he never puts it into practice. Let me tell you, I'm the best at doing things. So, sorry Husserl, but I'm not really interested in your "phenomenology." I'd rather go out and phenomenize.

Henri Bergson

Alright, here we go, folks! Today, we're gonna talk about a guy named Henri Bergson. Now, I gotta tell you, seems like not a very smart guy off the bat. Can't even spell his own name right. He's named after one of our greatest industry leaders and presidents, Henry Ford, and he can't even spell. Good luck living up to that.

Anyway, Bergson was a big fan of time, just like me. I have, and some may dispute this but they're wrong— I have the best times. I know how to have a good time. I love time, and time, I think, loves me. I mean, just look at me, and what do you think? Youthful, powerful, clearheaded. But then you look at someone like Sleepy Joe, and it's clear that time doesn't like everyone the same. But Bergson thought that time wasn't just a bunch of minutes and seconds ticking by on a clock. He thought it was more like this big flow. Like a river or something. And he said that we are constantly changing and adapting to that flow, but I don't know about that, folks. You look at me at a different point in time, and I'm still just as brilliant then. Can't change what you're made of, folks, one way or the other.

Trumping Philosophy | 145

But get this, folks: Bergson thought that our brains were actually holding us back from experiencing this flow. Like our brains are always trying to chop up time into little bits so we can understand it better, but the truth is, you can understand time just fine if your brain is good enough, and I would know. Bergson might be trying to come up with this new woke version of time, but I like it old-fashioned. 9 to 5, folks, 9 to 5.

But hey, I gotta give Bergson some credit. He did come up with this cool idea called "élan vital." Now, I think Elon is pretty vital to this country, but that's not what he means here. Basically, he thought that living things have this special force in them that makes them living, and it's why we grow and change over time. I mean, I don't know about you, but I think I've got a pretty strong élan vital, don't you? I've never changed, not once in my life. I came out of the womb with this exact hair. I'm not any different than I was years ago, and that's why the American people love me.

So, to sum up: Bergson was a French guy who thought time was like a river and our brains were like...I don't know, rocks or something, blocking us from experiencing the flow. But he did come up with this cool idea about élan vital, which is basically just a fancy way of saying "life force." And that's about all I've got to say about that, folks.

John Dewey

Alright folks, let me tell you about this guy John Dewey. He's a philosopher, or at least he thinks he is. He's another one of those pragmatism guys, but his ideas about education are all out of whack. But this Dewey guy thinks he's so smart. He's all about education and how we should learn by doing. He thinks we should get our hands dirty and actually experience things to really learn. Well, I don't know about you, but I prefer to learn from my mistakes by suing everyone who dares to criticize me. That's how you learn, folks. Dewey just doesn't have a clue about how these things work, and me tell you, he's no-Trump University professor, that's for sure.

And get this, Dewey thinks that democracy is more than just voting. He thinks it's about active participation and working together to solve problems. But let me tell you, nobody works together like me. Just look at my beautiful, amazing wall. It's big and beautiful, and we worked with Mexico and plenty of the Mexican people to do it. They're gonna pay for it one day, folks, just watch. It'll be great.

But back to Dewey. He also believes in social reform and making the world a better place. Now, that's all well and good, but let's be real here, folks. Making the world a better place is all about making America great again. And nobody can do that like me. Now, I like reform, things have to change in order for them to be better. In fact, when I first ran for president, it was with the Reform Party. But listen up Dewey, because you can't make your reform social. You can't just bring in socialism and expect it to fix everything. You'll be changing things, but you'll be making them worse! Ah, who am I kidding, what's the point in trying to talk to him? We all know these radical socialists don't think! Plus, I think he's dead, too.

So, you know, this Dewey guy just doesn't have a clue. His ideas about education just aren't there, and frankly, they sound a little bit— and I don't use this word lightly— woke. We gotta make sure our students are learning about how America is the oldest and greatest country on earth, and no amount of socialism is gonna get in the way of that.

Alfred North Whitehead

Alright folks, Alfred North Whitehead. Now, the last time I knew someone who named his kid North, that guy went way off the deep end, so I'm not sure I have a lot of confidence in Alfred's father. But hey, maybe the apple ended up falling real far from the tree and this guy turned out to be great.

So, this Whitehead guy, he's all about process philosophy, which sounds like a bunch of mumbo-jumbos to me. But guess what? Just like so many of the other people we've talked about, Whitehead's idea is just about change. Whoop-dee-do. You know, it really seems like these guys don't ever come up with anything new. They just repeat each other, much like the mainstream media. But this Whitehead guy thinks he's so smart for some reason. He's all about how reality is made up of experiences, again, nothing new here, folks. Well, let me tell you, I've built some of the most beautiful buildings this world has ever seen, and they're some of the most real things we have here. And that's not an experience, that's a building! So, take that, Whitehead!

And get this, Whitehead thought that those experiences were all connected to emotion. But let me tell you, nobody knows more about human emotion than me. I'm the best at it, folks. Just look at how I can fire people on national TV and still be loved by millions. That's emotional intelligence, folks.

In conclusion, this Whitehead guy may think he's all that, but let me tell you, nobody knows more about change, reality, and emotion than me. I'm the greatest, believe me. And if Whitehead wants to keep up, he better start building some beautiful buildings and making America great again like I did. Oh wait, he can't! I already did that!

Benedetto Croce

Alright folks, let me tell you about this guy Benedetto Croce. One hell of a name, really. Ben here was all about aesthetics, the nature of art and beauty. Well, let me tell you, nobody knows more about beauty than me. My beautiful wives, my beautiful children, my beautiful buildings. It's all just the best. And just look at my beautiful, tremendous hair. It's the most beautiful hair you've ever seen, believe me.

Ben was also big on art is a form of expression and creativity. Well, let me tell you, nobody knows more about expression and creativity than me. I can express myself like nobody else, folks. Just look at my tweets. They're the most creative and original tweets you've ever seen. I entertained millions, possibly billions, of people, and you know what? That's the secret to success. You wanna win the presidency? Make 'em laugh. Fastest way to the White House, believe me.

And get this, Croce thinks that history is the study of human values and culture. But let me tell you, nobody knows more about culture than me. I'm a cultured guy, believe me. I have all the best words, and I know all the best people. Nobody has more culture than me. And that's why I love this country so much, we have so much culture. All the other people and places are jealous of it, and that's why they say so many nasty things. But even so, they keep coming here. But we gotta be careful, folks, not to lose that culture. We want the right people coming here from the right places. And we want them to do it legally.

But back to Croce. Another big individual freedom guy, and let me tell you, no one is more individual and freer than me. You know, I've got all these charges and lawsuits, but they never could pin me down. Nothing sticks, and that's because when you're the president, you're basically the freest guy ever. What's more American than that? I'm basically America incarnates, folks.

So, Ben had some smart thoughts, really smart thoughts. Makes a lot of sense when you think about them in our time. We gotta protect our culture, and we gotta protect our freedoms.

Nishida Kitaro

Alright, next up is Nishida Kitaro. And let me tell you, he's got a funny name. I mean, Nishida? Is that like a new sushi roll or something? You know, it wouldn't surprise me, because this guy is from Japan, whereas I just learned, they actually put their names backwards. Nishida is the guy's last name! Get that! A whole family of sushi rolls!

So, Nishida was really into this thing called "basho" And you know what, folks? That sounds like a made-up word to me. I mean, what the heck is basho anyway? Is that like a new type of dance or something? I don't know, folks. But then Nishida talks about something called "absolute nothingness," which I think is a little easier to understand. Just look at everything Sleepy Joe has done in office. The grocery store, your bank account, patriotism. Absolute nothingness, just a sad state, really.

And then Nishida talks about something called "pure experience," which is really just a fancy way of saying "enjoying life." And you know what, I'm all about enjoying life. I have the best life, believe me. Nobody has a better life than me. He then talked about something called "self-awareness," and you know what, I'm all about being self-aware. I have the best self-awareness, believe me. No one is more self-aware than me. I'm so careful with my words, and I'm so humble about it. I know what my limits are— they're unlimited, by the way— and I respect everyone except for the losers and the failures and the nasty people out there who aren't worth a damn thing. Self-awareness, folks, gotta have it, gotta have it.

So, you know, I might not know about basho or whatever, but Nishida seemed to have the right idea about some of these more American ideas. Good thing he used some English words sometimes, or else no one would have ever known what he was saying.

Bertrand Russell

Alright folks, we're talking about this guy Bertrand Russell, a real math whiz apparently. Probably did almost as well on the SAT as me, which I took all by myself. I can count to a million in no time, folks. Nobody can count like me. No one has ever counted faster or higher than I have. You look at my billions of dollars and you say, "wow, I can't even count that high." Well guess what, folks? Donald J. Trump can.

But when Russell wasn't doing math, he was talking about something called "logical atomism." And you know what, folks? That sounds like a bunch of nonsense to me. I mean, how can atoms be logical? We already know that atoms are un-American, so there's no way they can be logical, because how can you be logical when you hate America. Makes no sense, folks, which isn't very logical of him.

But let's give Russell some credit, folks. He did win the Nobel Prize in Literature. And you know what, I'm all about winning prizes too. I have the best prizes, believe me. Nobody wins prizes like me, except for when they get stolen by the Radical Left. And you know what, literature is important too. I think we can all agree on that. Like I said, I've read all the books,

Trumping Philosophy | 155

and I gotta say, there are some good ones out there. Russell knew his stuff, for sure, and I think when all is said and done, he probably was a mixed bag. Let's just hope he stays in my lane.

GE Moore

Alright folks, listen up. We're gonna talk about a guy named GE Moore. Now, you might be thinking to yourself, "wow, this guy seems really credible. What's a more American name than GE?" And believe me, folks, that's where I was too. But it turns out that Moore here was not the founder of General Electric, but instead was some English guy who liked to hear himself talk. But you know what they say, if you can't dazzle them with brilliance, baffle them with bull. And let me tell you, Moore was a master of baffling. A masterbaffler if you will.

So, this guy Moore was into "naturalistic fallacy," which basically means that a lot of not very smart people often think that just because something is natural, doesn't mean it's good. Now that's an idea that I can get behind. All these Leftists with their kale and they're beyond burgers, I mean, doesn't anyone respect McDonald's anymore? Doesn't anyone respect America? You know, processed foods have been part of this country's fabric since the Industrial Revolution, and now you're telling me I need to eat some plant goo in order to save the environment. This is what we get with nasty ladies like AOC and the Green New Deal. One day you're eating a Big Mac like a real patriot, the next thing you're eating some soy thing. Sad!

Trumping Philosophy | 157

But wait, it gets better. Moore also had this thing called the "open question argument." Sounds like something you'd hear in a courtroom, right? And believe me, I've been in many courtrooms, and they're all weasels. Well, it's not much better. Moore was basically saying that if you can ask "is X good?" and it's an open question, then X isn't necessarily good. Wow, what a groundbreaking discovery. I'm sure nobody ever thought of that before. Real genius stuff right there.

But you know what's really funny? Despite all of Moore's fancy talk, he couldn't even define what "good" meant. Can you believe it? He spent his whole life talking about what's good and what's not, but he couldn't even give a straight answer. Reminds me of some politicians I know. Always talking, but never actually saying anything. You know what's good? I'll define it for you. America!

Anyway, that's GE Moore for you. A philosopher who couldn't even define the word "good." Maybe he should stop trying with all the big words and brush up on the basics. But hey, maybe I'm being too hard on the guy. After all, today he'd be against the radical leftist agenda. And isn't that what really matters? Not whether you're right or wrong, but whether you're on the right team.

Martin Buber

Alright, listen up folks, it's Martin Buber time. Some people say he was a philosopher, but honestly, I'm not so sure. He sounds more like a librarian to me. But hey, I guess if you like reading books and stuff, that's your thing. Just don't expect people to think highly of you— especially me!

So, Buber had this "I-Thou" relationship. Basically, he was saying that when we interact with other people, we should see them as equals, not just objects to be used for our own benefit. I mean, duh! Isn't that common sense? But I guess Buber thought he was the first one to come up with it. I guess before Buber, everyone was going around using each other as pawns and trying to get a one-up over each other. Sounds pretty cutthroat to me. Now, get this. Buber died in 1965, so it really took a while for those equal rights to get here. Civil Rights Act was 1964, folks, remember that. Coincidence? I think not!

But wait, it gets better. Buber also had this thing called the "I-It" relationship. And no, that's not some new social media app. You'd have to go to my new platform Truth Social for that, where you can find Truths from the best minds, really. People like me, and other fantastic people like Dan Bongino. We've made an account for Buber, and you can bet that he'll be here any day now. But Buber was saying that when we treat other people as objects, we're not really having a true relationship with them. Yeah, okay, Martin. You think that I don't have real relationship with some of these bimbos I meet? I'll remember that the next time I'm negotiating a big deal.

But you know what's really funny? Despite all of Buber's fancy talk about relationships, he couldn't even keep his own marriage together. That's right, folks, he got divorced twice! And this is the guy who's gonna tell us how to have meaningful relationships? Give me a break. Now, you might say, "Well, Don, you've been divorced twice," but what you have to understand is that that's because I'm just so popular. All these women, they're on me like flies, can't get enough of me. It's not my fault I needed to do what I needed to do. Buber, on the other hand, total loser, couldn't even keep one woman.

In the end, I think Buber was just a guy who thought too many people deserved too many things, like rights and all that stuff. He came up with all these fancy ideas about relationships, but he couldn't even make his own relationships work. Reminds me of some of my ex-wives, always talking about love and stuff, but they couldn't even stay married to me for more than a few years. It's about commitment, folks, and you gotta have it if you want to be a winner!

Wittgenstein

Alright folks, Wittgenstein, Wittgenstein. I wonder what type of guy he must be. Nothing about that name could tell us anything, of course! Although you might think what I was thinking, it turns out this guy is actually Austrian, which is really interesting. I thought they were all about boomerangs and kangaroos, not philosophy and stuff. Hard to understand them, too, so I'm not sure why this guy was so into word games, and in particular this one called the "language game." He was basically saying that language is like a game, with its own set of rules and meanings. Yeah, okay, Ludwig. Maybe you should stick to playing Scrabble. The only board game you good folks would ever need is Trump: The Game.

Now, Wittgenstein didn't actually explain any of the rules of this language game, but he did have another thing called the "picture theory of language." He was saying that language is like a picture that represents reality. So if I say "I'm a billionaire," that's like a picture of me being a billionaire? It just doesn't make any sense, because you see folks, just because you say something, doesn't mean its true. I mean, look at all these nasty people in the media saying things about me. All these women who say I did these things, it's just not true folks, and no amount of whining to the media or a jury will make them true. Try painting that, Wittgenstein! But you know what's really funny?

Despite all of Wittgenstein's fancy talk about language, he couldn't even communicate his own ideas clearly. That's right, folks, he wrote these long, convoluted books that nobody could understand. And to make things worse, he put them in German, which just doesn't make any sense at all! We get it! You know some big long angry-sounding words! Just put it in English so other people can read it! I think Wittgenstein was just a guy who liked to play word games. He came up with all these fancy ideas about language, but he couldn't even explain them in a way that normal people could understand. What a sham!

Heidegger

Alright, folks, now we have Heidegger, who sounds more like a guy who spent too much time in the woods talking to himself than a real philosopher. What's with the name, too? What was he digging for?

So, Heidegger had this idea called "Being," which honestly isn't that impressive. I've heard that word before. And I think it's older than some Guy who died in the 1970s. And it's a pretty simple word, one that even someone like AOC could understand. And it's a pretty simple explanation, too, because all Heidegger meant was that the universe is really big and real hard to understand. Big whoop, Heidegger. Take a hike. Oh, well, I suppose he already did. But wait, it gets better. Heidegger also had this thing called "Dasein." And no, that's not some new kind of yoga. He was saying that human existence is unique because we have this thing called "Being-in-the-world." But so what? Everything is in the world! That's what it means to be being in the world! Not very smart, let me tell you.

But you know what's really funny? Despite all of Heidegger's fancy talk about Being, he couldn't even keep his own personal life together. That's right, folks, he was a Nazi sympathizer! Can you believe that? This guy thought Germany was destined for glory, and that it was under attack by some very nasty people, and they had to do something about it. What a ridiculous thing to say, really. Everyone knows that that's America, not Germany! I think Heidegger was just a guy who liked to pretend he was smarter than he is. He came up with all these ideas about Being, but that didn't keep him from Being a Nazi. Ha! Reminds me of some politicians I know, always talking about how great they are but they can't even keep their own house in order. Sad!

Rudolph Carnap

Alright folks, we're gonna talk about this guy named Rudolph Carnap. Now, I know what you might be thinking. "Hey Don, how the hell can a reindeer do philosophy?" Well let me tell you folks, it turns out that this is a whole different Rudolph. Crazy, I know. Surprised me, too. But this Rudolph was into "logical positivism," which was about only statements that can be scientifically verified are meaningful. Uh, okay, Rudolph. I guess that means all those tweets I send out aren't meaningful? I beg to differ. Some of the best words ever written down.

And Rudolph also had this thing called "the verification principle." And no, that's not some new kind of lie detector. He was saying that the things you say only matter if you can observe them. Huh? I don't know about you folks, but I'm pretty sure there are things that are meaningful that can't be verified through a microscope. Take, for example, everything the Democrats do with ballots. They do it in the middle of the night when no one is watching, and you can't verify it, you just have to believe me. Does that not stand up to your principles, Rudolph? Shame. I always knew Santa was a communist.

But you know what's really funny? Despite all of Carnap's fancy talk about logic and positivism, he couldn't even make up his mind about what language he wanted to speak in. That's right, folks, he switched between German and English so much that people started calling him "Rudi." Now, I know a Rudy, and let me tell you, he did great things for this country, and more importantly, for me. Rudolph is clearly trying to piggyback off of that tremendous success after he's fallen out of favor with the public. They say they've moved him to fourth position in the sleigh line-up. Truly sad, truly sad!

Karl Popper

Okay, Karl Popper. Another Austrian guy, and apparently a British one, too. You know, I thought that was where Britain sent their prisoners, not the other way around. Very confusing, much like Popper! He had this idea called "falsification". Sounds like a fancy word for lying, doesn't it? Well, it's not much better. He was basically saying that the only way to test the truth of a statement is to try and disprove it. I guess that means I should try to prove myself wrong every time I say something? That's not gonna get me anywhere! You really wanna know what to do, folks? You gotta prove yourself right. If someone tries to do anything else, you gotta put up a fight. Show the world how much of a loser they are.

Popper wanted all of this to happen in what's called an "open society" where people can argue all they want. And folks, I really don't get this one. Why would you want the people you disagree with going around and saying all these nasty fake news narratives about you? What good would that do you? Looks like Popper is just buying into the radical left agenda.

But you know what's really funny? Despite all of Popper's fancy talk about falsification and the open society, he couldn't even make up his mind about whether he was a socialist or a capitalist. That's right, folks, he was all over the place. Reminds me of some of my opponents who can't decide whether they want to be left-wing or right-wing. You can't have wishy-washy people in Congress, folks. That's why they call it Washington. If they can't decide, that means they're part of the Left, folks, it's that simple.

Popper seemed to struggle with some basic ideas when it came to politics, and you just can't have that, folks, you can't have it. Maybe he should that falsification trick on himself so he can make up his mind!

Theodore Adorno

So, Theodore Adorno never had any fun in his life, a real boring guy. Didn't like anything. What a shame. He was all about fighting "the culture industry," which he said was the fact that the mass production of culture, like movies and music, was turning people into mindless consumers. Just not true, folks. There's lots of great stuff out there. Ever seen *Home Alone 2*? Best performance ever in there, believe me, Academy Award stuff.

He was also one of those radical CRT people, too, talking about how we need "critical theory" to figure out who is oppressed and who isn't. What a joke. You know, he might hate pop culture, but he'd probably love all this woke stuff that Disney is doing. I mean, what happened to movies like *Gone with the Wind,* folks? Back when everyone got along. We gotta go back, folks, gotta go back.

But you know what's really funny? He couldn't even make up his mind about whether he liked popular culture or not. I mean, come on, Theodore, do you want movies to be all woke like they are now, or not? Seems like those two just don't go together.

In the end, I think Adorno was just a guy who didn't like anything fun. Hated everything that makes our society work, and just wanted to complain about how everyone's oppressed. Well, Adorno, it's sounds like you're de-pressed, not op-pressed. Get it together. Sad!

Jean-Paul Sartre

Now we're gonna talk about this guy named Jean Paul Sartre, and let me tell you, big on existentialism. Real big on it. Thought a lot about existence. But let me tell you, John, I don't know what you think you need to know. We exist, right? Descartes said that earlier! You French guys really need to communicate better. It's probably because you speak a language that no one understands. English, folks, English.

But besides not being able to figure out whether he even exists, John was a big fan of authenticity. Loved showing off your true self. And folks, if I am one thing other than brilliant and rich and a genius and powerful and a great man and attractive and humble and tremendous and knowledgeable and literate and the greatest president the country has ever seen, I am authentic. That's what matters the most.

So, you know, John here might not have had the clearest idea about whether he was real, but he seemed to like when other people were real. And yeah, after all, how are you supposed to make deals when no one else is real? John might have been a little confused at times, but I think he's got the right spirit.

Hannah Arendt

Well, folks, let me tell you about this Hannah Arendt character. Some people say she was a philosopher, but honestly, she was just a total bore. She had all these ideas about politics and the nature of power, but who cares? I mean, I'm the President of the United States, I know more about politics and power than anyone. I HAVE more politics and power than anyone. And that's the truth!

And you know, it's real swell they're letting women do philosophy now, believe me. I love women, and I'm all for women. Truly beautiful creatures, most of them anyway. Some of them can even think pretty well, and that's how we get ones like Hannah. But here's the thing, folks, Hannah said some not very nice things that suggest she may not have liked me very much. Which is really a shame, folks. I love women, and women love me. Beautiful ones, anyway.

So Hannah was all about "the banality of evil." Can you believe it? She said that people like me, who do bad things, aren't even really evil, we're just banal. What a crock! I'm not banal, I'm the greatest President in history! No one is less banal than me! They look at me and they say "wow, so not banal. Not banal at all." That's a real quote, folks. So real even Rudolph would approve.

Anyway, Hannah Arendt wrote a bunch of books, but who cares? I've got Twitter! And she even had the nerve to criticize my buddy, Benjamin Netanyahu. Not cool, Hannah, not cool. Netanyahu's a great guy, believe me. Very Jewish. Probably knows more about it than anybody! Hannah just didn't have a clue.

Simone de Beauvoir

So, Simone de Beauvoir, huh? Some people say she was a philosopher, but honestly, she was just another feminist trying to stir up trouble. She had this whole idea about "The Second Sex," where she said women were oppressed by men. And believe me, folks, none of it is true. Women can have second sex whenever, just ask Stormy Daniels. And really, women have it great in America. Just look at my daughter Ivanka, she's a successful businesswoman and has never been oppressed a day in her life. Beautiful, too.

And then there's her whole thing about freedom. She said that freedom is something you have to fight for, but come on, folks, who needs to fight for freedom when you're already the leader of the free world? I've got plenty of freedom, believe me, and the other losers like Simone who complain just want to take away some of ours. And as for equality, we already have that. Women can do anything men can do. After all, men let her write her book, didn't they?

But get this - she had this whole relationship with Jean-Paul Sartre, and they were never even married. Can you believe it? What a scandal! As for me, I prefer to keep things traditional.

I've been married three times and have a beautiful wife, Melania. That's 3 for Don, zero for John and Simone. Total losers!

In the end, Simone de Beauvoir was just another feminist trying to shake things up, but sorry Simone, you can't shake up what's already great.

Willard Van Orman Quine

Well, let me tell you folks, Willard Van Orman Quine was a real egghead. He called himself a philosopher, but all he did was talk in circles. He had this whole thing about "ontology," which is just a fancy way of saying what exists and what doesn't. But look, let me tell you, it's really easy to tell what's real, and you don't need to use some fancy method. This country, it exists. Your favorite president, I exist. These witch hunt scandals? Don't exist! Votes for Joe? Don't exist! Just listen to me, folks, I'm the only one you can trust these days.

He also had this whole thing about "indeterminacy of translation," which is just another way of saying that people can't really understand each other. But come on, folks, I understand people just fine. And if they don't understand me, it's their loss. And you know what, if people can't understand each other, it's the Democrats' fault. They bring in the crime and the drugs, and those people speak languages that we don't have in America. You want to fix people not understanding things, Willy? Get them to speak plain English!

Willard Van Orman Quine just didn't have a clue, folks. No influence, no real ideas, it's all just things we've heard before. Sad!

AJ Ayer

AJ Ayer? What does the AJ stand for, Already Just a loser? This guy was a philosopher who thought he knew everything, but let me tell you, he didn't know anything. He was another one of these logical positivist people, and that's all you really need to know to see he's a total loser. You don't need to prove things; you just need to say them! And get this - he was British. I mean, really? You're gonna trust a guy from England to tell you what's true and what's not? They couldn't even beat us in a war. Sad!

But Ayer's biggest mistake was when he said that religious statements were meaningless because they couldn't be proven scientifically. Well, let me tell you folks, I believe in God, and I know millions of Americans do too. And our faith is meaningful, believe me. Just look at how many people showed up to my inauguration. That was a God-ordained event, believe me. Maybe that's what AJ stands for: Anti-Jesus!

So, we've got a Jesus hating Englishman who wants to come in here and tell us that we can't actually prove anything about anything. What a joke! You know what you *can* prove? The American Revolution!

Wilfrid Sellars

Wilfrid Sellars, folks. He was a philosopher, and let me tell you, he was a real piece of work. He had this whole thing about "linguistic behavior," which is just a fancy way of saying how we use language. But who cares about that, right? I use language just fine. In fact, I have the best words, believe me. I've read 'em all. But Sellars, he just wanted to complicate things, add more words in there. Because here's the thing, folks, Sellars was trying to come off as original when he never had a single original thought. Not one.

Sellars also had this whole thing about "the myth of the given," which is just another way of saying that you can't trust your own perceptions. But come on, folks, I trust my own perceptions all the time. Like when I look in the mirror and see the most handsome man in the world. That's not a myth, that's just the truth. You can ask any of the closest people around me and they'll tell you exactly what I want to hear. That's real loyalty, folks, and when you can't depend on your perceptions, you can always depend on the people who always agree with you.

But get this - Sellars was a professor at the University of Pittsburgh, which is one of the worst cities, let me tell you. Lotta Democratic votes coming out of there. Let me tell you, I won Pennsylvania big, and I mean big. But the Democrats found all these magical votes there.

In the end, Wilfrid Sellars was just another philosopher and just another Democrat. Never really made his mark on the world. What a loser. Sad!

John Rawls

Okay folks, we've got John Rawls, another John who just didn't have things together. He's got this whole thing called the "veil of ignorance," where you imagine you don't know anything about yourself or your position in society. I mean, I guess that's a good idea if you're a total fake and loser and you don't want to put in the work to be better, but if you're a winner like me, then why would you want to do that? Ignorance is what's ruining our country, folks, believe me. People need to wake up. I am fully anti-ignorance. You know they have ig-norance for when you don't know anything, but that means that I'm totally norance. Absolutely on board with it, folks.

But let's be real, Rawls was just jealous of people like me who are born into success. I mean, I didn't choose to be born into a wealthy family, but you know what I did choose? To make billions of dollars by being a part of that family. It's all about choice, folks, and playing the hand you're dealt. If my father wasn't wealthy, I just would've asked a different wealthy family member. It's not that hard, folks.

And Rawls also had this whole idea about "justice as fairness." But here's the deal— things aren't fair here at all. Totally unfair. Americans are being left behind, and I don't see Rawls saying anything about what Obama did to our great Rust Belt! If Rawls really wanted things to be fair, he'd be lining up behind me, but unfortunately, just like millions of other dead voters, he's supporting Sleepy Joe. Sad!

Thomas S. Kuhn

Okay folks, we've got Thomas Kuhn, the philosopher who came up with this whole idea of "paradigm shifts." He basically said that science isn't just about accumulating more and more knowledge, it's about changing the way we see the world. And you know what? I can relate to that, because I'm all about making big changes. I changed the way everyone saw things. I exposed the swamp and the elites for what they really are. No one knew before I came along. I came along and they said "Donald, we can't believe it!" and I said to them "you better believe it." Now they're out to get me again, and that's what makes thinkers like Kuhn so important.

But Kuhn was also a big future guy, because he said that science is never really objective, and that what we see as "facts" can change over time. And that's exactly right, folks. Sometimes the facts aren't the facts, and you gotta look at the alternative facts to get a clearer picture. And I love future guys, like that one with the rockets. Not Kim Jong-Un, the other one. Elon! That's it. Real smart guy, shoulda been on this list.

And Kuhn also had this whole thing about "incommensurability," where he said that different scientific theories can't be compared to each other because they're based on different assumptions. But folks, those assumptions are what make it easy to judge. Just look at me and Sleepy Joe. I assume that America is the oldest and greatest country on earth, but Sleepy Joe is just a loser and a hater who hates you and your country. You can still compare us and see that it's obvious I'm the better president; it's not even a question. Maybe Kuhn was right, we really are incomparable. What a shame, Joe, guess you're the "incommensurable" one!

Foucalt

Okay folks, we've got Michel Foucault, the French philosopher who was all about power and how it shapes society. But you know what? I don't think he really understood power. Because if he did, he would have realized that I am the most powerful person in the world, and that's just a fact. Foucault talked about how power is everywhere, and how it's not just something that the government has. Well, guess what? I am the government, and I am the most powerful person in the world. I mean, just look at the crowds at my rallies, folks. Nobody has more power than me. Foucault was all about how institutions and systems have the power; sounds like a load of critical race theory indoctrination to me!

Foucault also had this whole thing about "discourse" and how language is used to control people. But you know what? I'm the best at using language to control people. I mean, just look at how I get the media to cover my every move. They can't get enough of me, folks. And just look at my words on Twitter! Really brilliant stuff, unparalleled. Big word, I know, but it means "the best."

And then there's Foucault's whole thing about "panopticism," where he said that people are always being watched and controlled by the authorities. And you know, this is the one thing he got right. The deep state and the swamp, the Clintons and the Obamas, they spent years spying on us all, me especially. But when I was in office, you had nothing to worry about. No problems if you had nothing to hide.

But you know, the worst thing about Foucault is that he was trying to lower the age of consent. Can you believe it, folks? Foucault was real big on little girls and boys. What a creep. So Frisky Foucault may have been right about the deep state, but do you really want to associate with this guy? Give me a break.

Noam Chomsky

Alright folks, we got this guy Noam Chomsky, he thinks he's all smart with his linguistics and political activism. But let me tell you something, he's just a bigly overrated guy, and a major Leftist!

First of all, he's always talking about how language shapes the way we think and how we communicate. But let me tell you folks, nobody has a better way with words than me. I have the best words, the most beautiful words. My speeches are legendary. People love the way I talk. So much winning, believe me.

And then there's his whole thing about media propaganda and how it's used to control people. But let me tell you, nobody knows more about media manipulation than me. But Chomsky's got it all wrong. He thinks they're going after the Left, but they're really going after me!

And then there's his criticism of American foreign policy. Let me tell you something, folks: I'm making America great again all over the world. Nobody knows how to negotiate better than me. I'm winning so much; other countries are begging me to make deals with them. Chomsky calls me things like "fascist" and "war criminal," but the truth is, folks, you gotta make strong moves in order to win big. That's how you deal with other countries that want to take our freedom. No compromises. Sorry, Noam.

In the end, Commie Chomsky lives in his Radical Leftist bubble and doesn't know how the real-world works. A total failure.

Jurgen Habermas

Alright folks, we got this guy Jurgen Habermas, he thinks he's all smart with his theories on communicative action and the public sphere. But let me tell you something, he's just a bigly overrated guy. He's always talking about how communication is the key to solving social problems. But let me tell you folks, nobody communicates better than me. I have the best tweets, the most beautiful words. I'm a master communicator, believe me. A masternicator. Nothing better than that, folks.

And then there's his whole thing about the public sphere and how it's important for democracy. But let me tell you, nobody knows how to rally a crowd better than me. I can draw huge crowds at my rallies, and they love me. I'm the king of the public sphere, folks. As for democracy? As long as my crowd gets their way, it's gonna be just fine. I'm the best at democracy, I'm so good at it that the other team has to cheat to "win."

Habermas kinda falls apart with his criticism of capitalism, folks. And here's the problem with that. There are two ways of doing things: you got capitalism, which makes people like me rich, and you got socialism, which makes everyone in for a really bad time, believe me. We can't let people take over our country with those ideas, folks.

And you know what's really funny about this guy? In Mexican, his name means "have more." That's right, folks. There's the truth of it. He just wants more of your stuff, so the next time you see Habermas, make sure to tell him "No!" which is how you say "No" in Spanish.

Sir Bernard Williams

Alright folks, we got this guy Sir Bernard Williams, another one of these English university types. Let me tell you, all these philosopher academic guys can't compare to the staff at Trump University. Our philosophy department is unbelievable. In fact, this book will be added to the curriculum very shortly.

Now, Williams talks a lot about morality and how it's important for our lives. But let me tell you something, folks: nobody has more morals than me. I'm the most moral person you'll ever meet. I always do what's right, believe me. I have the most morals, the most rights, the most good out of all the people who have ever been president. My administration was the most successful and scandal-free in this country's history.

And then there's this whole thing about personal identity and how it's related to our memories and experiences. But let me tell you something, folks: I have the best memory, the most incredible experiences. Nobody has a better personal identity than me. Nothing beats the Trump name, let me tell you. Can't do it. And Williams was really insistent on consequences, that's right folks, consequences. He said we can't always see them, but let me tell you, I always know what's going to happen when I do something. And I never face consequences. Never. They're all on my side. And I think Williams would be too, because guess what? He hated utilitarianism just as much as I do. It doesn't protect people's rights, he says, and that tells me he's a real smart guy. Really gets it. Gotta has rights, folks, gotta have 'em. You know what we get when there's no rights? That's right, wrongs.

So, Williams had a pretty clear idea of where things were at. He'd probably be a great Trump University employee. Really great stuff, we hire the best people, and Williams is I think one of the best.

Jacques Derrida

Alright folks, we got this guy Jacques Derrida. Guess what! Another French guy! Who would've thought? Now, Jack is real into deconstructionism, which is just a long, and frankly, unnecessary and ugly word that just means taking this apart. Believe me, no one takes things apart more than I do. Give me a deal, an Executive Order, anything. I'll dismantle it, folks. I'll break it down.

Now, it's kind of ironic that Jack used such a big and ugly word to describe such a small and beautiful thing, because he didn't think that words were actually clear in their meaning. Well, I got bad news for you, Derrida, if you don't understand some basic words like bigly and covfefe, that means you're dumb. What a shame.

Derrida also talks about how there's no real center or fixed meaning to things. Now, that's just a bunch of baloney. If you look at a map of the center of the world, New York City, what do you see at the center of it? That's right, Trump Tower. Nothing more central to the city, and frankly, the country.

In the end, Jacques Derrida is just another French guy with big words and no real solutions. But me? I'm a winner. I'm a doer. I'm getting things done, folks. And nobody does it better than me. Believe me.

Richard Rorty

Alright folks, we got this guy Richard Rorty, a philosopher from the Left. But let me tell you something, he's not as smart as he thinks he is. He likes to talk a lot about truth and how it's all relative, but let me tell you something, folks: there's only one truth, and it's that I'm the best. He thinks that he can twist the truth around to fit whatever narrative he needs, but just listen, folks, if I say it's wrong, then it's wrong. It's that simple.

He's also all about this idea of "postmodernism," which is just a fancy way of saying that he wants to tear down the old ways of thinking. Now, here's the thing, I'm all about tearing things down, but it's the new ways we gotta focus on. All this radical leftist CRT woke stuff needs to be broken down and replaced with the old ways. We gotta go prepostmodern, folks, prepostmodern.

Rorty also talks about how we need to focus on social progress and helping people who are marginalized. But let me tell you something, folks: I've done more for marginalized communities than any other president in history. Nobody has done more for the African American community than me. Just look at my African American friends, they love me, aren't they

Trumping Philosophy | 196

great? Same with the Hispanics, best Taco Bowls in the country come from Trump tower.

In the end, Richard Rorty is just another ivory tower intellectual who doesn't understand the real world. Do we really want to live in a world where we tear all of our institutions down? If not, folks, you know what to do.

Robert Nozick

Folks, we got this guy Robert Nozick, a philosopher from the right. He's all about individualism and liberty and all that good stuff. The guy cared a lot about the importance of property rights and how the government shouldn't interfere with them. And let me tell you something, folks: nobody knows more about property rights than me. I mean, I've owned buildings all over the world. Nobody has more property than me. I've got property in good countries and socialist countries alike, and let me tell you, you gotta love the good countries.

But Nozick also believes in something called the "minimal state," which is just a fancy way of saying that the government should stay out of people's business. And let me tell you something, folks: nobody loves the government more than me. I mean, I am the government. And nobody is better at interfering in people's business than me. But it's not for everybody, folks, so don't worry. The good people, we can leave them alone, but if we're going to protect true patriots from the woke left, we've gotta do something.

Nozick also talks about the importance of free markets and how they're the best way to allocate resources. And look, no one knows the markets better than me. I know them so well; I know what's going on with them weeks before the public does. I'm just that smart.

You know, Nozick talks all about being from the right, but the truth is, he's not MAGA. He's just a RINO who doesn't want to do what it takes. SAD!

Saul Kripke

You know, folks, I've been hearing a lot about this guy Saul Kripke. Now, I watch a lot of TV, folks, a lot, I'm very well educated. And I gotta say, there's another Saul guy that really seems like he's got the right idea. Very smart lawyer, loves the Constitution. But Kripke, well he's all talk. He's always going on about "necessary truths" and "possible worlds" and all this other stuff that nobody really understands. There's only one world, folks, and that's the American world.

I mean, who needs all these "rigid designators" and "causal chains" and whatever else he's talking about? It's just a bunch of gobbledygook. But you know what? Maybe that's the point. Maybe he's just trying to make himself seem important by making everything sound so complicated. I mean, I know I like to simplify things for people. I like to make things easy to understand. That's what the people want.

So Kripke, he was too into words and not enough into ideas. He just didn't have a clue. What a shame, folks, what a shame.

David Kellogg Lewis

David Kellogg Lewis? Never heard of him. Is he related to Jerry Lewis, the great comedian? Maybe not as funny, but who knows?

Anyway, what my aides tell is me is that Lewis was a philosopher who liked to talk about possible worlds. I mean, who cares about possible worlds? I prefer to focus on the real world, and that's what I'm doing as a president, making America great again! We've got enough problems here. We've got the crime and the drugs and the CRT and the fraud, and if we start worrying about other worlds, we aren't going to fix what we've got going on at home.

But if Lewis wants to talk about possible worlds, let him do it. He's probably some kind of weirdo who likes to live in his own imaginary world. Maybe he's trying to escape from reality, like those losers in San Francisco and Chicago who do drugs and crime. You know what's real? Real people's pocketbook. That's what we should be talking about. How to make more money, how to keep our economy strong, how to create jobs for Americans. That's the kind of stuff that really matters.

According to Lewis, there are many possible worlds, and some of them are more real than others. Now, I can at least get behind that some things are more real. You lovely people, for instance, you're real Americans, unlike a lot of those Communist losers in DC and our inner cities!

So, in conclusion, David Kellogg Lewis is a weirdo who likes to talk about possible worlds. Let's leave him in his imaginary world and focus on the real world, where I'm making America great again!

Peter Singer

Alright, let's talk about this guy Peter Singer. He's an Australian philosopher and he's got some pretty wild ideas. First of all, he's all about this thing called animal rights. He thinks that animals should have the same rights as humans. Can you believe that? I mean, what's next? Dogs voting? Cats driving cars? We already have cows like Rosie O'Donnell on TV! It's crazy!

And that's not even the worst of it. Singer also believes in something called effective altruism. Basically, it means you should give all your money away to charity. Can you believe it? He thinks you should just hand over your hard-earned cash to complete strangers, who are probably just gonna spend it all on drugs and stuff like that! No way! The reason I have all this money is because I know how to spend it, folks, that's the truth of this country. There's no better investment than spending millions on legal fees to fight an election result, evidence be damned. Stimulates the economy, helps everybody. If anything, it's altruistic!

And it's not just animal rights and effective altruism that Singer is into. He's also big on utilitarianism. But here's the real kicker here, folks, because that utilitarianism doesn't apply to babies, which he doesn't think are real people. Now, a liberal baby I can maybe see, but otherwise? They're our future, folks, they're our future. Gotta sign 'em up to vote for our great Republican Party.

So yeah, Peter Singer. He's a real piece of work, but that's what you get from the liberal elite today. I'll enjoy my Trump steak while he cries over his vegan soy whatever!

Paul Woodruff

Let me tell you something about Paul Woodruff, folks. He's a tremendous guy, really fantastic. Believe me, nobody knows more about things than Woodruff. He's like the Einstein of philosophy. You thought E = MC squared was good? Just wait till you hear about Woodruff's ideas. It's like E = MC squared squared.

Woodruff is like the superhero of philosophy. He talks a lot about Plato and Aristotle and all those real ancient old guys we discussed at the beginning, and he's got a real knack for it, let me tell you. He was really into talking about the philosophy of theater, folks, have you heard of this, the philosophy of theater? It's basically, well, I don't want to get ahead of myself, but it's basically when you think real deeply about plays and stuff. Now, believe me, I know plays, I'm a New Yorker after all. Woodruff knows almost as much as me about it.

Now, let me give you an example of Woodruff's brilliance. He talks about something called "virtue ethics." Sounds pretty boring, right? But wait till you hear this. He says that being virtuous is like being a superhero. Can you believe it? I love superheroes, folks. So, according to Dr. Woodruff, if you're virtuous, you're basically like Superman or Wonder Woman. Incredible! And we all know that I'm the most virtuous person out there, I have the most virtues. Just a great collection of them. So, really, what Woodruff is saying, is that I've got basically every superpower.

And here's the best part, folks. Dr. Woodruff doesn't just talk about philosophy in some boring academic way. No, sir! He brings it to life. It's like watching a Batman movie, but with deep thoughts instead of explosions. I can't believe I waited until now to get to this guy; it would've made reading all this other philosophy stuff earlier so much better. It's tremendous.

So, in the end, Woodruff is a great guy, great guy. Has a lot of ideas, and I think if we were to meet, he'd like me quite a lot, just like everybody else. Maybe he'd give me those superpowers he promised me!

Robert Kane

Folks, let me tell you about this guy, Dr. Robert Kane. First thing's first, that sounds like a fake name. Now, believe me, I know all about having a unique name, but Robert Kane just sounds like some alter ego, like a name given so he can infiltrate us. Who gave him the name? China perhaps? Who knows?

But probably not China, because let me tell you, Dr. Kane has some really wild ideas that I don't think China would like very much. He's all about something called "libertarian free will." Sounds like a mouthful, right? But really all it means is that we're the ones in charge of our own choices, and they're only determined by what we want. I gotta say, Kane gets it. I'm in charge of a lot of things, believe me. Businesses, pageants, Americas. I know all about being in charge, and that starts with being in charge of myself.

So, according to Dr. Kane, we can just do whatever we want, whenever we want. It's like being the boss of your own reality TV show. You can fire people, you can hire people, you can even build a wall if you feel like it. But here's the kicker, folks. Dr. Kane doesn't just talk about this stuff. He actually comes up with these crazy scenarios to prove his point. He's like the master of philosophical thought experiments. One of his favorites is the "golf ball experiment." He says that if you have a bunch of golf balls in a jar and you want to take one out, you can just reach in and pick any ball you want. And that's what I do, folks. I have the best golf courses, I play the best golf, and I have the best balls.

So the next time you're going to make a decision, make sure you check in with Robert Kane, because if you think you don't have what it takes, Kane will tell you that you do. Just pick the golf ball, folks, that's all you have to do.

Robert Solomon

Folks, let me tell you about this guy, Dr. Robert C. Solomon. Now, right off the bat, I gotta say, he's got a lot of names. Robert C. Solomon sounds like he's part of some secret society or a long-lost relative of King Solomon from the Bible. It's tremendous. Maybe he even has a treasure map hidden somewhere. Who knows?

So, what's Dr. Solomon all about? Well, hold onto your hats, folks, because he's all about emotions. That's right, emotions. Now, you might be thinking, "What's the big deal? We all have emotions, right?" But let me tell you, Dr. Solomon takes emotions to a whole new level. The biggest emotions, the best emotions. He says that emotions are like these powerful forces that shape our lives. It's like having your very own emotional superpower. And, you know, I got all those superpowers from Woodruff, so maybe Dr. Solomon says that I get the best emotions too. Maybe I'm like the Emotion-in-Chief or something. That's got a nice ring to it, don't you think?

But wait, it gets even better, folks. Dr. Solomon was real big on existentialism like some of these other guys, but the deal is, he talked about what it has to do with responsibility, and let me

Trumping Philosophy | 209

tell you— it's a lot! He said that we're responsible for our own existence and our choices, and that's the truth, folks. If you succeed, you gotta take the credit for it. If you fail, it's your responsibility to find someone to blame and fire. That's your responsibility, folks, and it's how you get ahead.

I can just imagine Dr. Solomon and me sitting down for a philosophical discussion. We'd be like two big personalities, going back and forth, trying to outdo each other with our words. It would be like a battle of the philosophies. The biggest show on television, folks, much better ratings than any other network!

So, to sum it up, Dr. Robert C. Solomon really knew what he was talking about with emotions and existentialism, and he did it much better and much more successfully than many others. Groundbreaking stuff, really, and I'm proud to call him one of mine!

Did this book help you in some way? If so, I'd love to hear about it. Honest reviews help readers find the right book for their needs.

For every review I'll give my daughter Izzie a piece of candy! Help make Izzie happy and kindly leave a review. Thank you!

ABOUT THE AUTHOR

Chat TCT is the brainchild of Thomas C. Turner, Jr. He is a graduate of the University of Texas at Austin, where he majored in Philosophy, and a graduate of the University of Texas at Austin Law School, where he majored in truancy. Turner practices in the field of oil and gas law. When not in the office, he can be found fly fishing in Montana, Colorado and Louisiana. His true love is his wife, Kathleen, and their daughter Elizabeth.

Chat TCT utilized Chat GPT in the formation of Trumping Philosophy, however, Chat GPT did not write the text. Rather, the artificial intelligence was used to gather factual data on the philosophers included in this book. Turner then honed that data into the text you've just read. Please note, like the narrator of the text, artificial intelligence programs often times incorporate false data with factual data ("hallucinations"). We have chosen to leave such instances in the text as it more humanizes the experience.

Finally, a very brilliant young ghost writer participated in the writing of Trumping Philosophy. His epic comedic wit can be found throughout. The ghost writer, true to form, prefers to remain anonymous so as not to sully his good reputation.

<u>JOIN MY MAILING LIST</u> for updates on future works by Chat TCT. Next up: Trumping Mathematics: the Greatest Mind Explains the Greatest Cosines

Join here: subscribepage.io/8szqpX

Printed in Dunstable, United Kingdom